It's another Quality Book from CGP

This book has been carefully written for 10-11 year olds.

There's lots of stuff to learn in the Year 6 Maths Programme of Study. Happily, this CGP book explains it all as clearly and simply as possible.

What's more, it's perfectly matched to the new National Curriculum making it ideal for the SATS in May 2016 and beyond.

What CGP is all about

Our sole aim here at CGP is to produce the highest quality books — carefully written, immaculately presented and dangerously close to being funny.

Then we work our socks off to get them out to you — at the cheapest possible prices.

Contents

Section Five — Algebra

Section Six — Measurement

Section Seven — Geometry

Section Eight — Statistics

Published by CGP

Editors:
Katie Braid, Katherine Craig, Ben Fletcher, Rob Harrison, Sarah Pattison, Camilla Simson.

ISBN: 978 1 84762 193 1

With thanks to Karen Wells and Mary-Ann Parsons for the proofreading.
With thanks to Jan Greenway for the copyright research.

Printed by Elanders Ltd, Newcastle upon Tyne.
Clipart from Corel®

Based on the classic CGP style created by Richard Parsons.

About This Book

This Book has All the Topics for Year 6

By the end of Year 6, you should be able to do all the maths in this book.

Each page covers a different topic, with examples to help explain the maths.

This book covers the Attainment Targets for Year 6 of the 2015 National Curriculum. The topics covered are roughly equivalent to the old Levels 4-6.

Examples are colour-coded to show the difficulty of problems in a topic.

EXAMPLE:	EXAMPLE:	EXAMPLE:
Easy	Harder	Challenge

At the end of each section are practice questions.
You can see what you know and what you don't know.

These questions are colour-coded too, to help you pick which ones to tackle.

Key:
- Easy Start
- Getting Harder
- Challenge

This Study Book has a matching Question Book.
It's got questions on all the topics and some practice tests too.

There are Learning Objectives on All Pages

Learning objectives say what you should be able to do.
Use the tick circles to show how confident you feel.

You can use the tick boxes for ongoing assessment to record which attainment targets have been met. Printable checklists of all the objectives can be found at www.cgpbooks.co.uk/primarymaths.

Tick here if you think you need a bit more practice.

If you're really struggling, tick here.

Tick this circle if you can do all the maths on the page.

"I can multiply a four-digit number by a two-digit number."

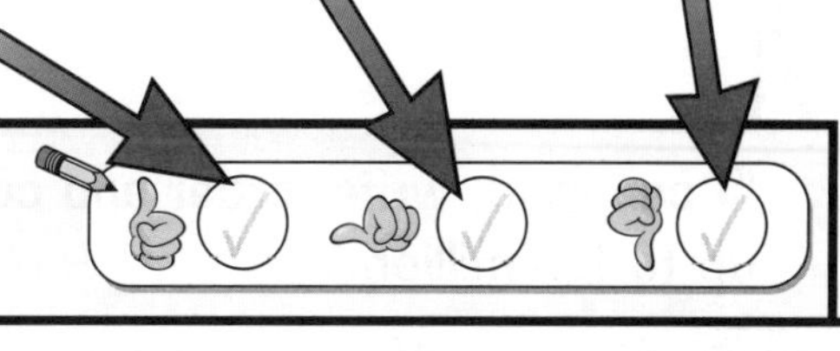

Place Value in Very Large Numbers

8-digit Numbers are in the Tens of Millions

This number is huge — the digit furthest to the left is the ten millions. It's said as: "Seventy four million, two hundred and fifty nine thousand, three hundred and eighty six."

ten millions → **74 259 386** ← units

millions, hundred thousands, ten thousands, thousands, hundreds, tens

Put spaces before the last three digits and the last six digits to make it easier to read.

You can partition it into:
70 000 000 + 4 000 000 + 200 000 + 50 000 + 9000 + 300 + 80 + 6.

EXAMPLES:

In January, the planet Zog is about nine million, four hundred and two thousand, six hundred and forty miles from the Sun.
Write this out as a number.

nine million → **9 402 640 miles**

four hundred and two thousand — six hundred and forty

Put a < or > in the box to make this correct. → 1 402 640 ☐ 1 420 322

The first two digits are the same.
The ten thousands digit is larger in the second number, so the answer is  <.

Put these numbers in ascending order: 4 509 460, 1 402 640, 4 028 640.

The millions digit is smaller in the second number, so that number will be first.

The millions digit is the same in the first and third numbers, so move on to the hundred thousands digit.

4 509 460
1 402 640
4 028 640

The hundred thousands digit is smallest in the third number, so that number will come next.

The first number comes last in the list.

Answer: 1 402 640, 4 028 640, 4 509 460.

"I can read, write, order and compare numbers up to ten million."

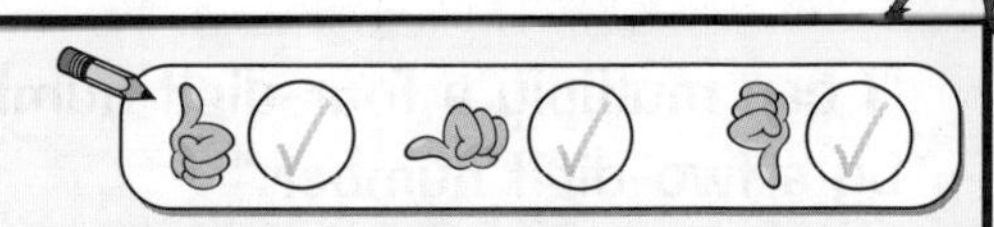

Rounding Whole Numbers

Rounding Whole Numbers

You might have to round a number to the nearest ten, hundred or thousand.

The Rounding Rules

1. The number lies between two possible answers. You have to decide which one it's nearer to.
2. Look at the digit to the right of the place you're rounding to — the DECIDER.
3. If the decider is 5 or more then round UP. If the decider is less than 5 then round DOWN.

So, if you round to the nearest thousand, the decider is the hundreds digit...

Th	H	T	U
3	5	6	1

...here it's a 5, so you'd need to round up to 4000

EXAMPLES:

a) Lasso Les the pest catcher trapped 680 499 insects in one day. How many is 680 499 to the nearest thousand?

680 499 is between 680 000 and 681 000.
The decider is 4 so round down to 680 000.

b) In an insect outbreak, giant insects caught 1235 people. How many is 1235 to the nearest ten?

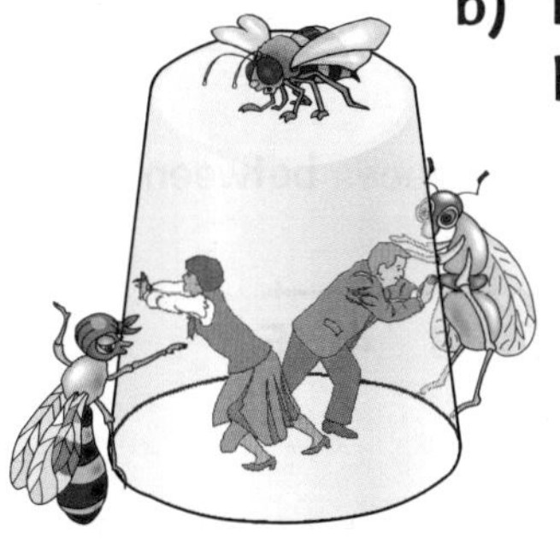

1235 is between 1230 and 1240.
The decider is 5 so round up to 1240.

c) After the outbreak, Lasso Les caught 41 256 909 insects. How many is 41 256 909 to the nearest ten million?

41 256 909 is between 40 000 000 and 50 000 000.
The decider is 1 so round down to 40 000 000.

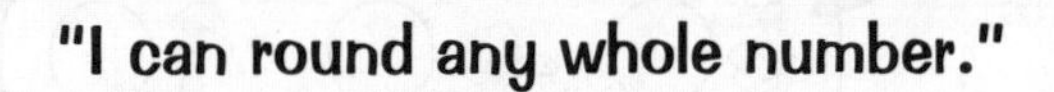

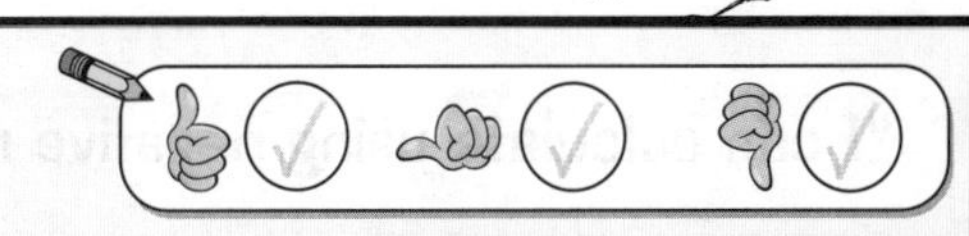

Calculating With Negative Numbers

Adding and Subtracting Negative Numbers

Number lines are really useful for problems that have negative numbers in.

Just draw part of the number line.
Then COUNT ON or BACK to get the answer.

EXAMPLE: What is -4 + 6?

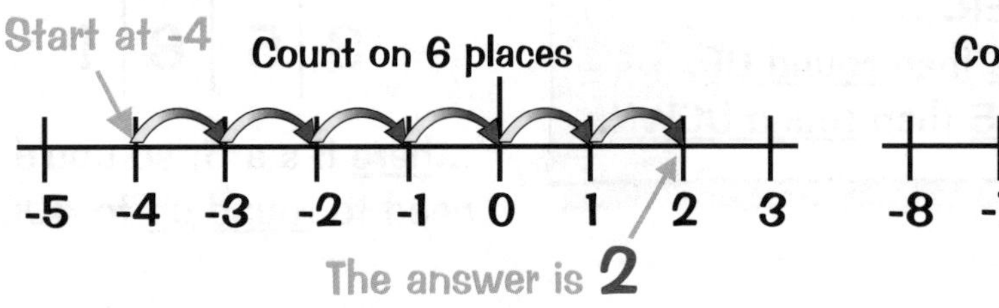

EXAMPLE: Work out -4 – 3.

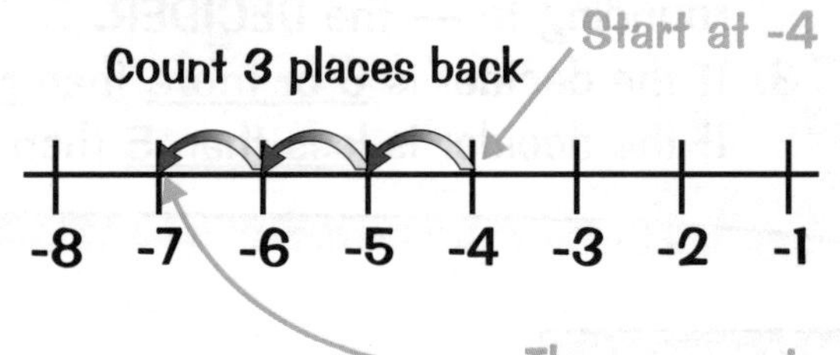

Working Out Differences

EXAMPLE:

The temperature inside Jo's igloo was -14 °C. She filled it with fish, and the temperature rose to 4 °C. What was the change in temperature?

Do a quick sketch of the number line. Mark the two temperatures on it, then count how many degrees there are between them.

It's often easiest to count the places to zero, then the number of places after zero and then add them together.

There are 14 places between –14 and 0. There are 4 places between 0 and 4.

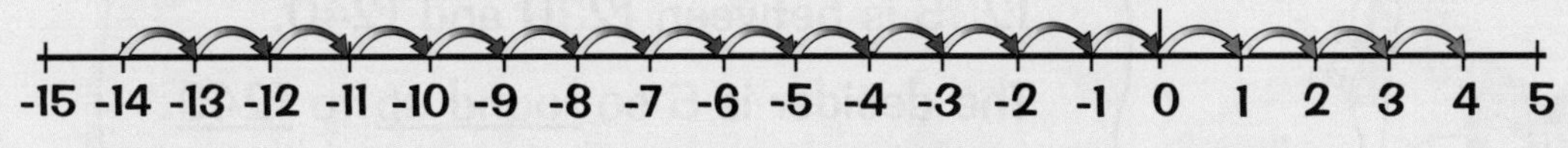

So the temperature rose by 14 + 4 = 18 °C.

EXAMPLE:

The temperature in Svalbard is -53 °C.
The temperature in Abisko is -17 °C.
Find the difference between these temperatures.

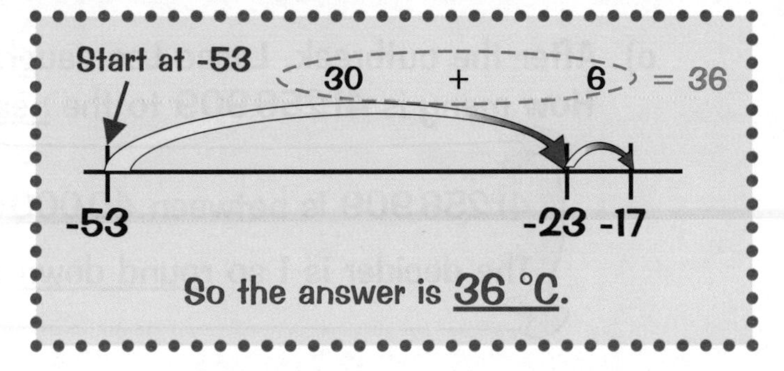

So the answer is 36 °C.

"I can calculate using negative numbers."

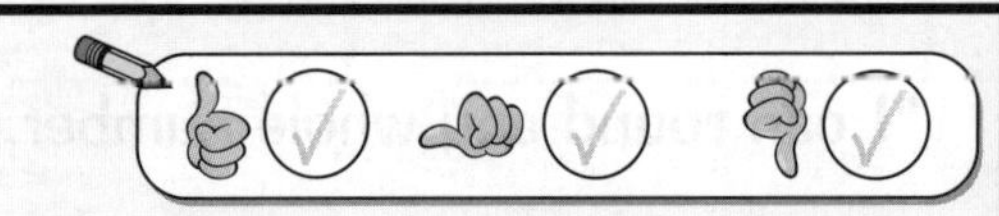

Solving Number Problems

Don't Be Put Off By Lots Of Words

You might get a wordy question where you have to decide what maths to do. It doesn't mean it's going to be hard maths — it's probably maths you've done lots of times.

EXAMPLE:

If you have a negative amount in the bank, you owe the bank that much (a shame really).

Dai's bank account had –£156 in. He added £200 into his account. How much was then in the bank account?

This is "what is –156 + 200?" in disguise. So, sketch a number line. Do it in two parts: from –£156 to £0, and from £0 to the final answer.

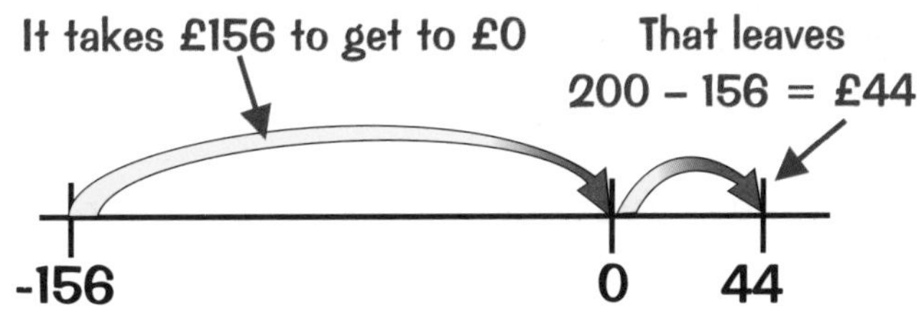

So the answer's £44. Don't forget the £ sign.

Drawing a Diagram Might Help

EXAMPLE: Dai works in an underground car park. All the floors are 10 m apart. Dai's office is on floor –4. He takes a lift up to –3 to fix a light. Then he goes down in the lift to floor –12 to fetch another light bulb. Finally he gets the lift to his office. How far has he travelled in the lift?

Draw a diagram of all his journeys.

He starts here, on floor –4.

You know that each floor is 10 m above the one below.

Find the distance travelled on each leg of his journey. Then add them up to find the total distance he travelled.

10 + 90 + 80 = 180 m

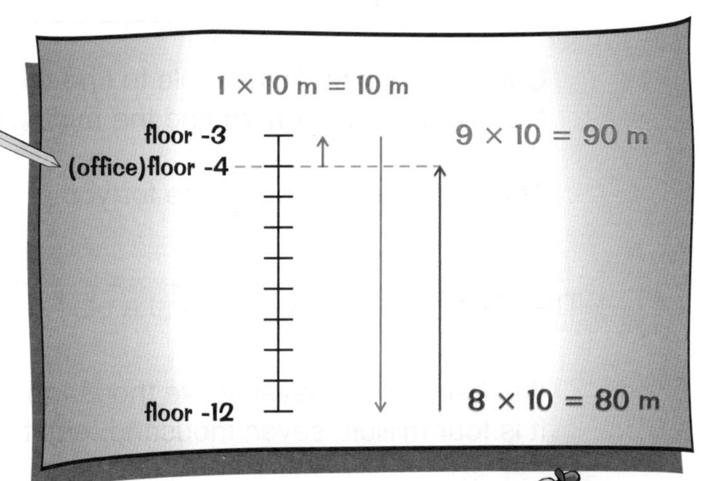

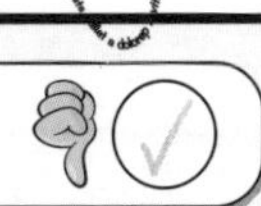

"I can solve number problems."

Practice Questions

Start off with the **green** questions — they're the easiest ones.
The **blue** ones are a bit harder, and the **pink** ones are the hardest.

1 23 162 870 vehicles drove along one busy road this year.

a) What is the value of the 1 in this number?

b) Round this number to the nearest thousand.

2 This table shows the temperatures in three people's fridges.

a) What is the difference in temperature between Costas' and Daniel's fridges?

b) What is the temperature in Eva's fridge, to the nearest 10 °C?

c) The temperature in Eva's fridge gets 11 °C colder. What temperature is it now?

Fridge	Temperature
Eva's	6 °C
Costas'	1 °C
Daniel's	–9 °C

3 The table below shows the temperatures at midday and midnight in four towns.

Town	Temperature at midday (°C)	Temperature at midnight (°C)	Temperature difference (°C)
Normalsville	22	4	18
Heaton	39	26	
Nippiham	4	–7	
Chillbeck	–6	–14	

Copy and complete the table to find the difference between the midday temperature and the midnight temperature for each town.

The first one has been done for you.

4 The distance all the way around a planet has been worked out.

It is four million, seventy five thousand and seventeen metres around the equator.
It is four million, seven thousand, eight hundred and sixty metres around the poles.

a) Write these distances in numbers.

b) Which distance is shortest — around the equator or around the poles?

c) Round the distance around the poles to the nearest ten thousand metres.

Written Multiplication

Long Multiplication

Do a quick estimation before you start:
$3151 \times 23 \approx 3000 \times 20 = 60\ 000$
The real answer must be bigger than this.

EXAMPLE: What is 3151×23?

You're multiplying by a two-digit number.
This looks tricky but all you need to do is partition this number: $23 = 20 + 3$.
Work out 3151×20 and 3151×3 separately, then add them together.

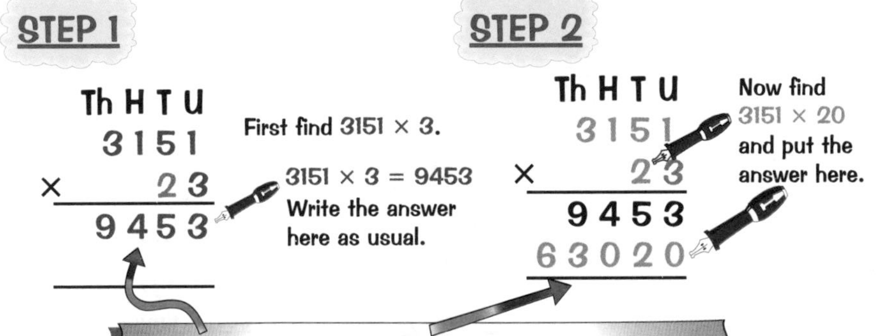

STEP 3

Add to get the final answer.

	Th	H	T	U
	3	1	5	1
×			2	3
	9	4	5	3
6	3	0	2	0
7	2	4	7	3

3151×3

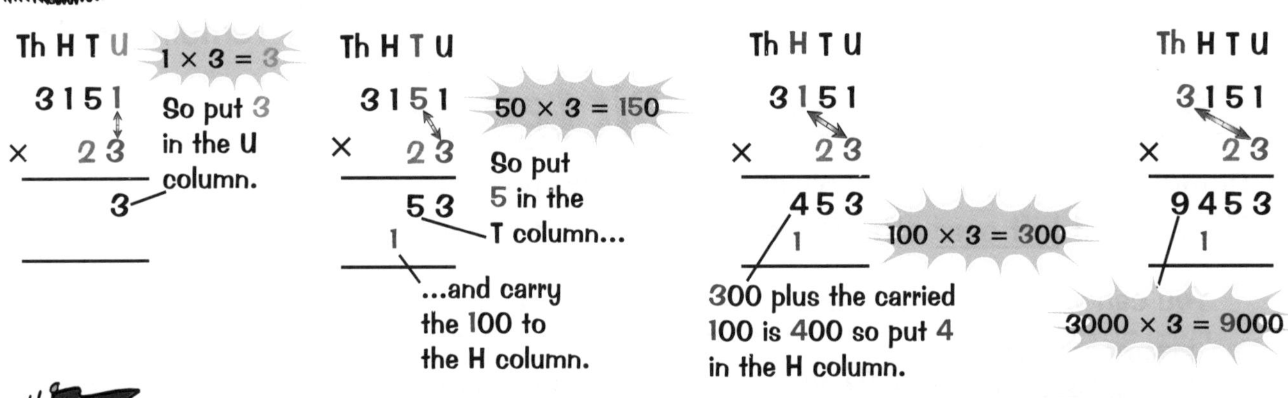

3151×20

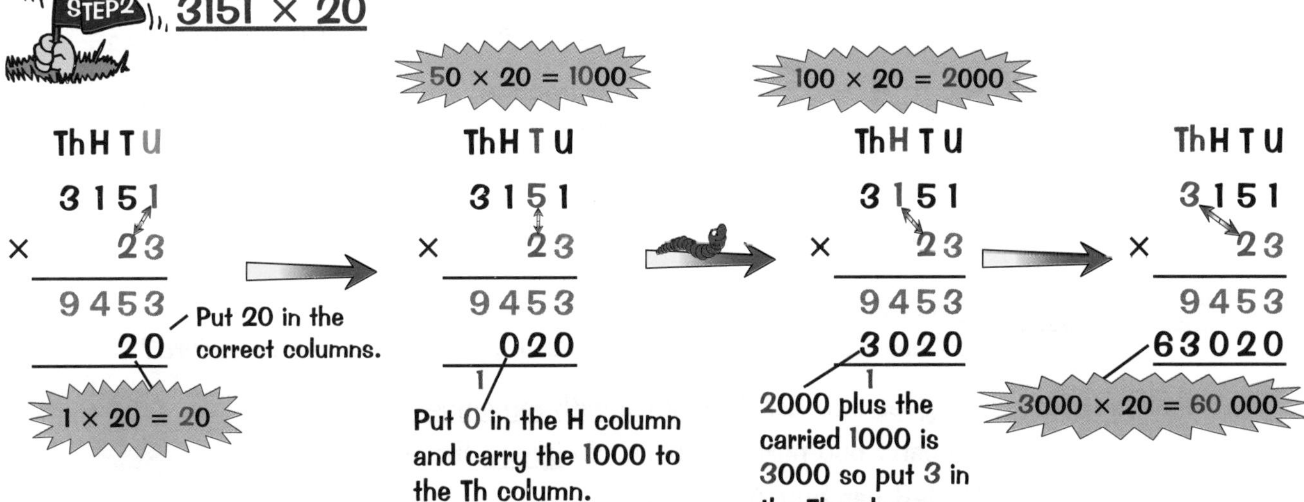

"I can multiply a four-digit number by a two-digit number."

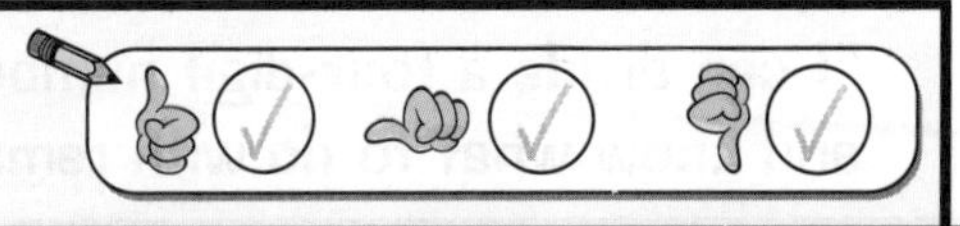

Written Division

Long Division

EXAMPLE: Find 3927 ÷ 12.

(1)

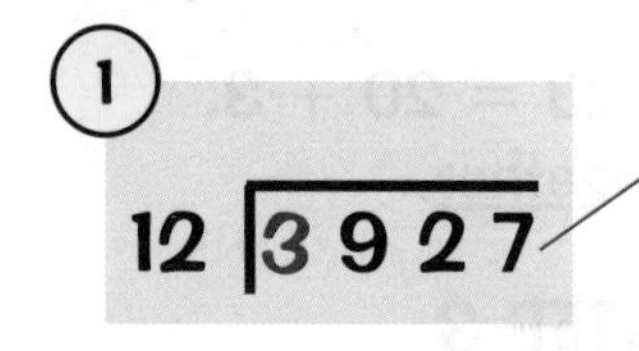

Big number goes inside.
12 into 3 doesn't go.
Look at the next digit.

(2)

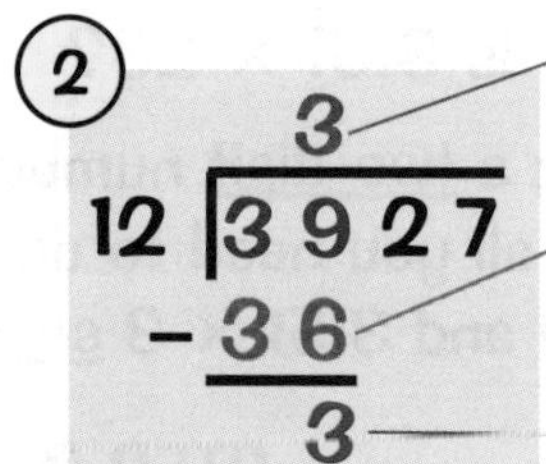

12 into 39 goes three times. So put a 3 above the 9.
3 times 12 is 36. So take away 36 from 39 to get the remainder.
Remainder

(3)

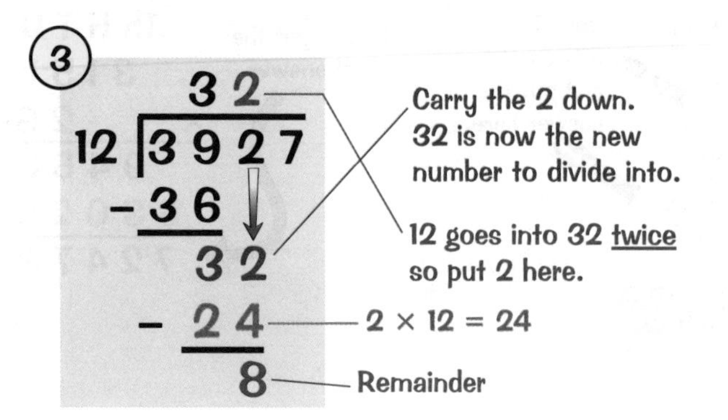

(4)

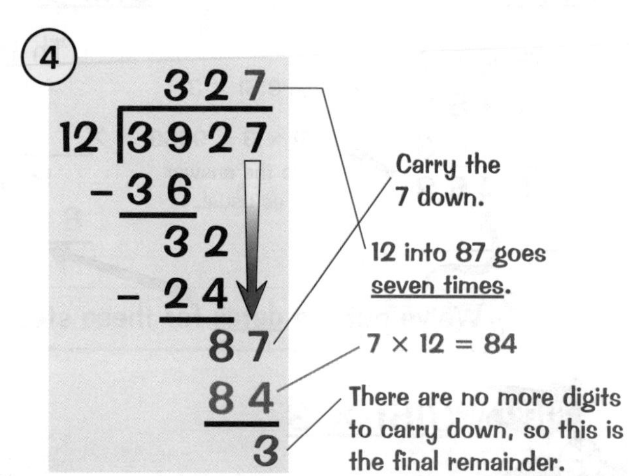

The answer is 327 remainder 3.

The Remainder is the Bit Left Over

Sometimes one number won't divide perfectly by another.
The amount left over after the division is called the remainder.

You can write the remainder in a few different ways.

EXAMPLE: 4 into 47 goes 11 times with remainder 3

So 47 ÷ 4 =
- 11 r 3 as a number.
- $11\frac{3}{4}$ as a fraction.
- 11.75 as a decimal.

The number on the bottom of the fraction needs to be the number you were dividing by.

Sometimes you'll need to round the answer to a whole number.

EXAMPLE: Sproutsicles cost 30p for a pack of 4.
Jeff has £1.27. How many packs of sproutsicles can he afford?

ANSWER: 30 goes into 127 four times with remainder 7.
He can't buy part of a pack, so ignore the remainder.
So Jeff can buy 4 packs.

"I can divide a four-digit number by a two-digit number and know what to do with remainders."

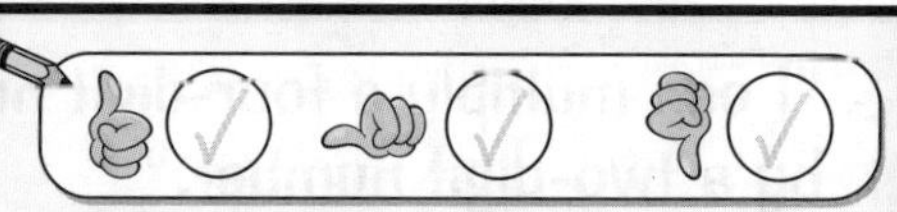

Mental Maths

Solving Problems in Your Head

The trick to working something out in your head is to do it in steps.

EXAMPLE: Kelly is 17. Her Dad says, "To work out my age, double Kelly's age and then add 27." How old is Kelly's Dad? Work it out in your head.

Work out the calculation you need to do in numbers: $17 \times 2 + 27$

STEP 1
Work out double 17. You can partition to make this easier. →
17 = 10 + 7
Double 10 = 20
Double 7 = 14
20 + 14 = 34

STEP 2
Now add 27 to 34.
Add 20 first, then 7. →
27 = 20 + 7
34 + 20 = 54
54 + 7 = 61

Write down the final answer. → Kelly's Dad is 61 years old.

Calculating with Big Numbers

To make adding and subtracting large numbers easier, partition the numbers.

EXAMPLE: What is 15 623 + 3250?

Partition 3250 to 3000 + 200 + 50
15 623 + 3000 = 18 623
18 623 + 200 = 18 823
18 823 + 50 = 18 873 → = 18 873

Partition and add the thousands, hundreds, tens and units separately.

Use exactly the same method for subtracting.

If you have a multiplication or division with big numbers, make them easier first.

EXAMPLES:

a) Work out 1200×8

Make 1200 a hundred times smaller. → 12
Then do $12 \times 8 = 96$
Then make the answer 100 times bigger.

96 → 9600

b) What is $32\,000 \div 8$?

Make 32 000 a thousand times smaller.
Then do $32 \div 8 = 4$
Then make the answer 1000 times bigger.

4 → 4000

"I can solve number problems and do calculations with large numbers in my head."

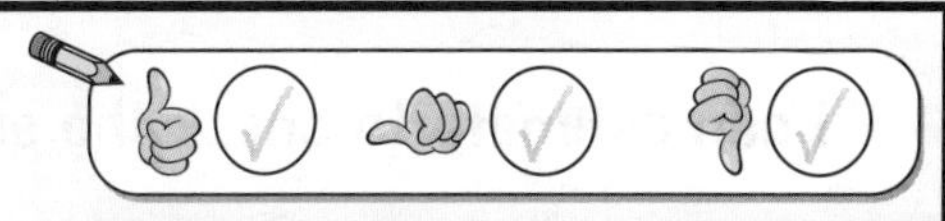

Estimating and Checking

When You Estimate, Use ≈ Instead of =

When you estimate things, use a bendy equals sign like this:  It means "is approximately equal to".

That's "is about" to the rest of us.

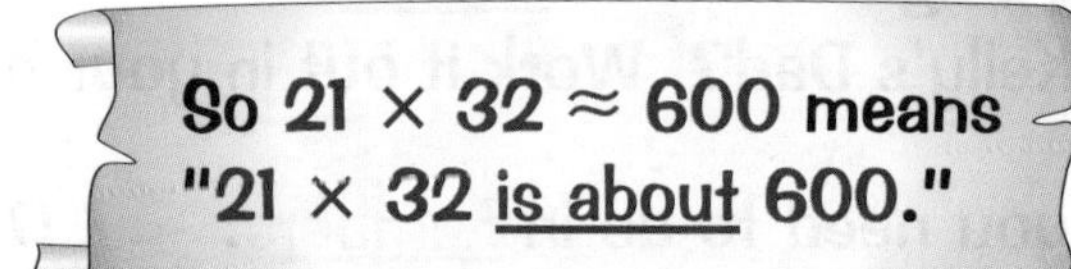

Bessie flies 9.81 km every second.
How far does she travel in 8.6 seconds?

The exact distance she travels is 9.81×8.6 km

9.81×8.6 is approximately equal to 10×9, which is 90 km.

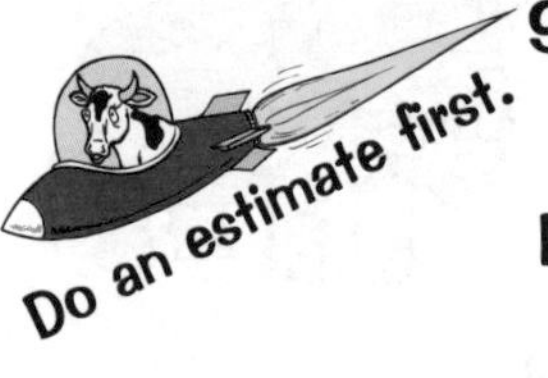

In symbols, that's $9.81 \times 8.6 \approx 10 \times 9 = 90$ km

So you know the answer is going to be somewhere near 90.

The answer should be a bit less than 90, because you rounded both numbers up.
If your answer isn't a bit less than 90, try again.

Find Two Numbers the Answer Lies Between

Sometimes it's good to do two easier calculations first.
You can work out two numbers that your answer must lie between.

EXAMPLE: Estimate $30.2 \div 4$.

30.2 is between 28 and 32,
so $30.2 \div 4$ is between $28 \div 4 = 7$ and $32 \div 4 = 8$
$30.2 \div 4$ is somewhere between 7 and 8.

These are good numbers to use because they both divide exactly by 4.

Always round to numbers that make the calculation nice and easy.

"I can estimate to check the answer of a calculation."

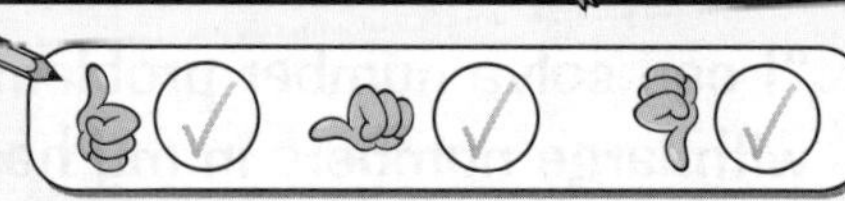

BODMAS

Always do Calculations in a Certain Order

In some calculations, there's more than one thing to do.
If you want to find 2 × 5 + 8, what do you do first? Multiply or add?

Luckily, there's a rule about the order to do things: BODMAS

B Brackets (see below)
O
D Division
M Multiplication
A Addition
S Subtraction

So for 2 × 5 + 8 or 8 + 2 × 5 you'd do the multiplication first, then the addition. The answer is 18 both times.

Brackets tell you which Step to do First

Some number sentences have brackets in.
The brackets show you which bit to do first.

4 ÷ (3 – 1) = ?

This means do the subtraction first: 3 – 1 = 2
Then do the division: 4 ÷ 2 = 2

EXAMPLE: Magic Martin has 10 apples. He makes 4 of them disappear.
He then halves the number of apples left.
Which of these number sentences shows what Martin has done?

10 – 4 ÷ 2 = 8 (10 – 4) ÷ 2 = 3 10 – (4 ÷ 2) = 8

Martin takes away 4 apples, then halves the number of apples.

Subtraction normally comes after division.
But Martin subtracts first, so there must be brackets around the subtraction.
So the answer is (10 – 4) ÷ 2 = 3.

"I know what order to do things in a calculation."

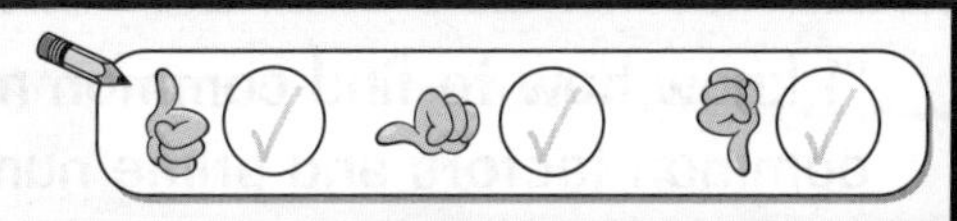

Multiples, Factors and Primes

Finding Common Multiples

A common multiple of two numbers is a number that's a multiple of both numbers. You can find them by listing times tables.

EXAMPLE: Find a common multiple of 4 and 6.

1) Write out the 4 times table... (Go up to 5 × 4 to start with.) → 4 8 12 16 20
2) ...then the 6 times table. → 6 12 ...
3) Look out for a number that's in both lists. When you find one, it's a common multiple. (There are lots, but you only need one for this question, so stop here.)

So a common multiple of 4 and 6 is 12.

Finding Common Factors

The factors of a number are whole numbers that divide exactly into that number. Common factors are factors that are shared by two or more numbers.

EXAMPLE:

The number 8 has factors 1, 2, 4 and 8.

The number 12 has factors 1, 2, 3, 4, 6 and 12.

So 1, 2 and 4 are common factors of 8 and 12.

Prime Numbers Only Have Two Factors

A prime number is a number that has exactly TWO FACTORS: 1 and itself.

EXAMPLE: The only numbers that multiply to give 23 are 1 and 23. 23 only divides exactly by 1 and 23, so it's prime.

1	**(2)**	**(3)**	4	**(5)**	6	**(7)**	8	9	10
(11)	12	**(13)**	14	15	16	**(17)**	18	**(19)**	20
21	22	**(23)**	24	25	26	27	28	**(29)**	30
(31)	32	33	34	35	36	**(37)**	38	39	40
(41)	42	**(43)**	44	45	46	**(47)**	48	49	50
51	52	**(53)**	54	55	56	57	58	**(59)**	60
(61)	62	63	64	65	66	**(67)**	68	69	70
(71)	72	**(73)**	74	75	76	77	78	**(79)**	80
81	82	**(83)**	84	85	86	87	88	**(89)**	90
91	92	93	94	95	96	**(97)**	98	99	100

All the circled numbers in this grid are prime numbers.

1) 1 is NOT a prime number — it doesn't have exactly 2 factors.
2) All prime numbers end in 1, 3, 7 or 9. 2 and 5 are the exceptions.
3) 2 is the only even prime.

BUT not all numbers ending in 1, 3, 7 or 9 are prime.

"I know how to find oommon multiples, common factors and prime numbers."

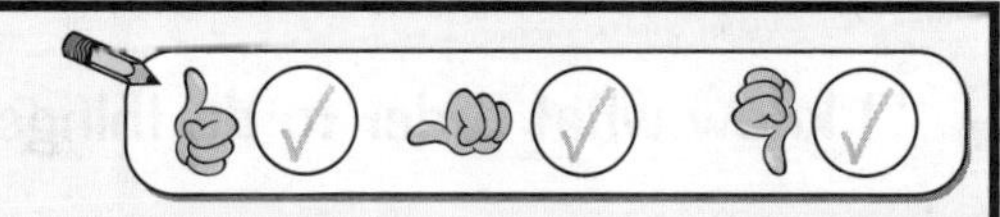

Solving Calculation Problems

Some Problems Can Be Quite Wordy

EXAMPLE:

It takes 14 bats to make one bowl of bat soup. Bats come in packs of 3.
Betty wants to make 2 bowls of bat soup. How many packs of bats does she need?

Betty needs 14 × 2 = 28 bats to make 2 bowls of soup.
There are 3 bats per pack, so to find the number of packs she needs, divide by 3.

28 ÷ 3 = 9 remainder 1

If Betty buys 9 packs, she will get 9 × 3 = 27 bats.
That isn't enough.
So to get 28 bats, she needs to buy 10 packs.

Break Calculations into Easy Steps

Sometimes you have to do more than one calculation to solve a problem.
Just read the question carefully and work out what steps you need to do.

EXAMPLE: Tuna cakes cost 56p each. Chocolate-coated snails cost 19p each.
Adil buys 5 cakes and 9 snails with a £5 note.
How much change does he get?

1. Find out how much 5 cakes cost.
   $56 \times 5 = 280$
   5 cakes cost 280p.

2. Find out how much 9 snails cost.
   $19 \times 9 = 171$
   9 snails cost 171p.

3. Find the total cost.
   Add the two costs together
   $280 + 171 = 451$
   So the total cost is 451p.

4. Find the difference between £5 and the cost.
   Change the pounds to pence.
   Subtract 451.
   $500 - 451 = 49$
   The amount of change is 49p.

"I can work out what calculations I need to use to solve a problem."

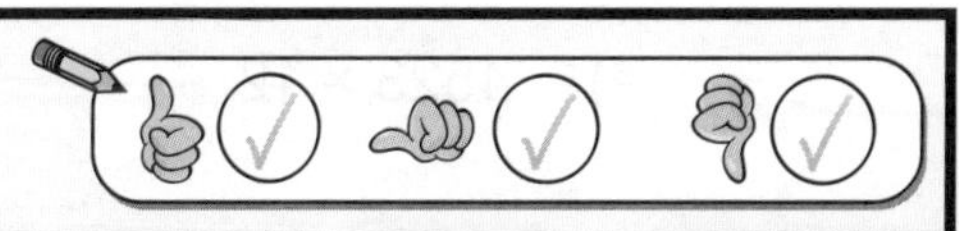

Practice Questions

Start off with the **green** questions — they're the easiest ones.
The **blue** ones are a bit harder, and the **pink** ones are the hardest.

1 Estimate 28.8 + 71.1 by rounding.

2 Find a common multiple of:

a) 8 and 12 b) 3 and 5 c) 6 and 9

3 Is 53 a prime number?

4 What is 45 ÷ 7? Write the remainder as a fraction.

5 What are the common factors of 16 and 28?

6 Estimate 22.5 ÷ 3 by finding two numbers that the answer lies between.

7 Guy calculates that 8.9 × 11.7 = 114.13.

Use rounding to estimate the answer to 8.9 × 11.7
and say whether you think Guy's answer is right.

8 Work out:

a) 6 ÷ 2 + 4 b) 6 ÷ (2 + 4) c) 6 + 2 × 4

9 Calculate:

a) 4523 × 12 b) 1595 × 24

Practice Questions

10 Work these calculations out in your head:

a) 27 310 + 3660 b) 12 692 – 4200

11 Dave has 16 fish. Charlotte has double the number of fish that Dave has.

How many fish do they have all together? Work it out in your head.

12 Write down all the prime numbers between 35 and 55.

13 Larry earns £1200 every month.

How much does he earn in six months? Work it out in your head.

14 Work out:

a) 6354 ÷ 11 b) 3145 ÷ 14

15 Phil drives 49.6 km every hour.

a) Estimate how far he travels in 2.7 hours.

b) Will the real answer be greater or smaller than the estimate?

16 Carol has 15 cakes. She eats 3 cakes and divides the rest among her 4 friends.

Which of these number sentences shows what Carol has done?

a) 15 ÷ 4 – 3 b) (15 – 3) ÷ 4 c) 15 – (4 ÷ 3)

17 Plastic pipes cost £3 for a box of 8.

a) Anja has £19. How many boxes of pipes can she buy?

b) James needs 29 pipes to make his lobster costume.
How many boxes does he have to buy?

Simplifying Fractions

Equivalent Fractions are Equal to Each Other

Equivalent fractions look different from each other, but are really the same.

For example $\frac{1}{2}$ and $\frac{4}{8}$ are equivalent fractions.

You can use fraction bars and see that the same amount is shaded.

Simplifying — Divide the Top and Bottom

Simplifying a fraction means making an equivalent fraction with the smallest numbers possible.

You just divide the numerator (top number) and denominator (bottom number) by the biggest common factor — that's the biggest number that goes into both.

$$\frac{16}{40} \xrightarrow{\div 8} \frac{2}{5}$$

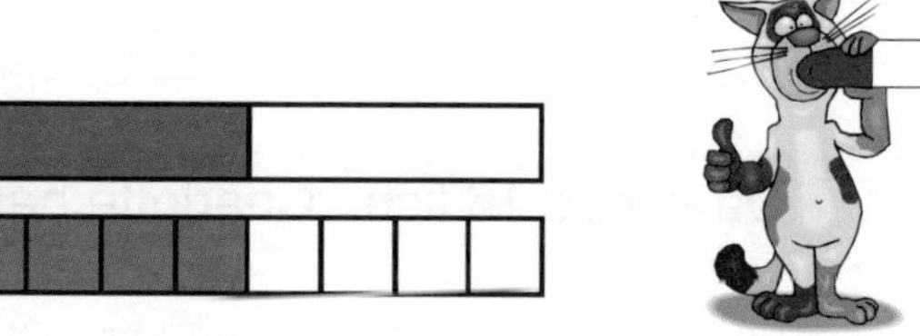

With big numbers, you can do it in stages.

When you answer a question with a fraction, always give the simplified answer.

You Might Need the Denominators to Match

When you work with fractions, it often helps if they all have the same denominator.

EXAMPLE: $\frac{3}{8}$ and $\frac{1}{12}$ have different denominators. Find equivalent fractions with the same denominator.

First, pick a common multiple of both denominators. Start by listing their times tables.

Write out the 8 times table...	8	16	24	32...
...and the 12 times table.	12	24	36	48...

So a common multiple of 8 and 12 is 24.

Then, find equivalent fractions for each, with the common multiple as the denominator.

The new denominator for both fractions is going to be 24.

24 is 8 × 3, so multiply by 3.

$$\frac{3}{8} \xrightarrow{\times 3} \frac{9}{24}$$

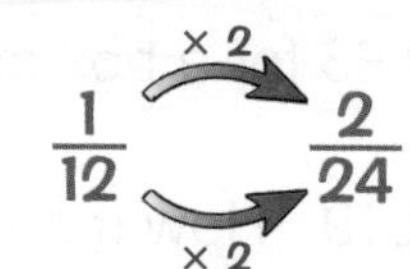

24 is 12 × 2, so multiply by 2.

$$\frac{1}{12} \xrightarrow{\times 2} \frac{2}{24}$$

Answer: $\frac{9}{24}$ and $\frac{2}{24}$

"I can simplify fractions. I can write equivalent fractions with the same denominator."

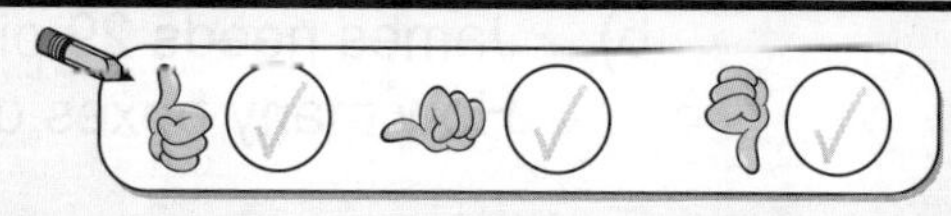

Ordering Fractions

Putting Fractions in Size Order

If the denominators are the same... ... just compare the numerators.
The bigger the numerator, the bigger the fraction.

If the denominators are DIFFERENT... ... make them the same by finding equivalent fractions — see page 16. Then compare the numerators.

EXAMPLE: Order these fractions from smallest to largest: $\frac{1}{3}$, $\frac{3}{4}$ and $\frac{3}{12}$.

1: Decide on a common denominator. You need a number that's a multiple of all your denominators. 3, 4 and 12 all have 12 as a multiple, so use that.

2: Make equivalent fractions that have your common denominator. $\frac{1}{3} \xrightarrow{\times 4} \frac{4}{12}$ $\frac{3}{4} \xrightarrow{\times 3} \frac{9}{12}$ ($\frac{3}{12}$ already has 12 as its denominator.)

3: Write out all the fractions and compare their numerators. $\frac{4}{12}, \frac{9}{12}, \frac{3}{12}$ 9 is larger than 4. 4 is larger than 3.

So from smallest to largest, the order is $\frac{3}{12}, \frac{4}{12}, \frac{9}{12}$

Now change the fractions back to the ones in the question. → $\frac{3}{12}, \frac{1}{3}, \frac{3}{4}$

Ordering With Fractions Bigger Than 1

Order improper fractions (fractions greater than 1, e.g. $\frac{15}{8}$) just like proper ones. Make equivalents with a common denominator, then compare their numerators.

You can order mixed numbers by converting them to improper fractions.

EXAMPLE:

Order these fractions from smallest to largest: $1\frac{2}{5}, \frac{13}{10}, 1\frac{1}{4}$

1) Convert them all to improper fractions: $1\frac{2}{5} = \frac{5+2}{5} = \frac{7}{5}$, $\frac{13}{10}$, $1\frac{1}{4} = \frac{4+1}{4} = \frac{5}{4}$.

2) Find a common denominator and write equivalent fractions: $\frac{28}{20}, \frac{26}{20}, \frac{25}{20}$

3) Order them: $\frac{25}{20}, \frac{26}{20}, \frac{28}{20}$ then put them in their original form: $1\frac{1}{4}, \frac{13}{10}, 1\frac{2}{5}$

"I can compare and order fractions, including fractions greater than 1."

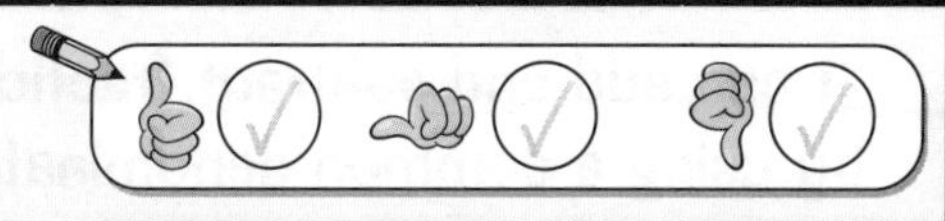

Adding and Subtracting Fractions

Make Sure the Denominators are the Same

You can only add or subtract fractions with the same denominator.
That means you often have to find a common denominator for your fractions first.
Then you add or subtract the numerators only (leave the denominator alone).

EXAMPLE: What is $\frac{1}{5} + \frac{1}{3} - \frac{1}{6}$?

First find equivalent fractions with the same denominator for each.

30 is a common multiple of 5, 3 and 6, so use 30 as a common denominator.

$$\frac{1}{5} = \frac{6}{30} \quad (\times 6) \qquad \frac{1}{3} = \frac{10}{30} \quad (\times 10) \qquad \frac{1}{6} = \frac{5}{30} \quad (\times 5)$$

Now add and subtract the numerators to get the answer:

$$\frac{1}{5} + \frac{1}{3} - \frac{1}{6} = \frac{6}{30} + \frac{10}{30} - \frac{5}{30} = \frac{6 + 10 - 5}{30} = \frac{11}{30}$$

You Can Add and Subtract Mixed Numbers

Turn mixed numbers into improper fractions before adding or subtracting them.

EXAMPLE:

What is $5\frac{1}{6} - 2\frac{5}{6}$?

Convert the mixed numbers to improper fractions:

$$5\frac{1}{6} = \frac{(5\times6)+1}{6} = \frac{31}{6}$$

$$2\frac{5}{6} = \frac{(2\times6)+5}{6} = \frac{17}{6}$$

These fractions already have a common denominator.

$$\text{So } 5\frac{1}{6} - 2\frac{5}{6} = \frac{31}{6} - \frac{17}{6} = \frac{31-17}{6} = \frac{14}{6} = \frac{7}{3}$$

Simplified by dividing top and bottom by 2.

$\frac{7}{3}$ is an improper fraction, so change it into a mixed number.

$$\frac{7}{3} = \frac{3+3+1}{3} = \frac{3}{3} + \frac{3}{3} + \frac{1}{3}$$

$$= 1 + 1 + \frac{1}{3} = 2\frac{1}{3}$$

"I can add and subtract fractions by using a common denominator."

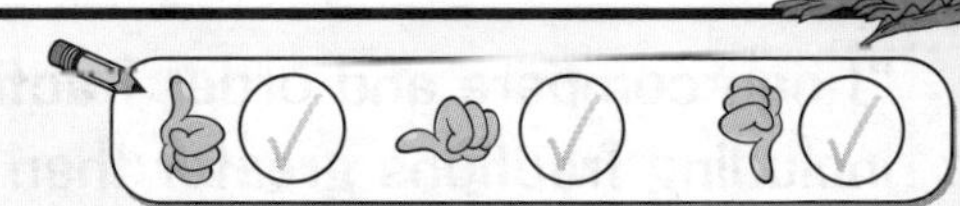

Multiplying Fractions

Multiply The Top And Bottom Separately

To multiply fractions:

1) Multiply the top numbers.
2) Multiply the bottom numbers.
3) Cancel down if it needs it.

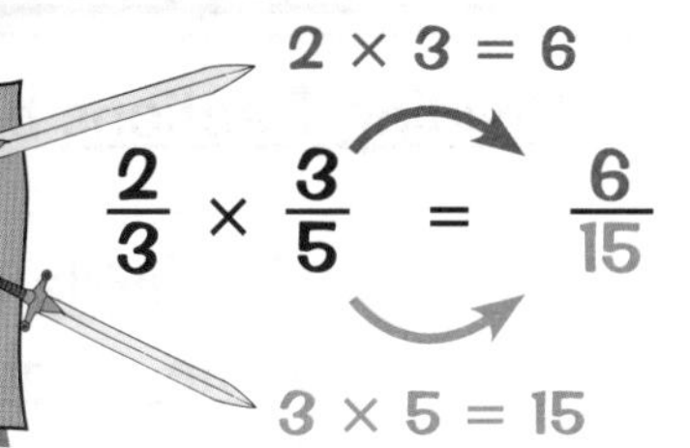

$\frac{2}{3} \times \frac{3}{5} = \frac{6}{15}$

Fractions Multiplied Together Get Smaller

EXAMPLE: What is $\frac{1}{2} \times \frac{1}{2}$? That's half of a half.

Multiply the numerators together and multiply the denominators together.

So: $\frac{1}{2} \times \frac{1}{2} = \frac{1 \times 1}{2 \times 2}$ and the answer is $\frac{1}{4}$.

Here it's shown on a fraction bar:

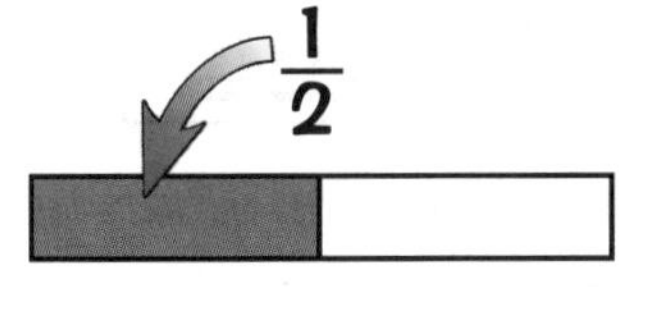

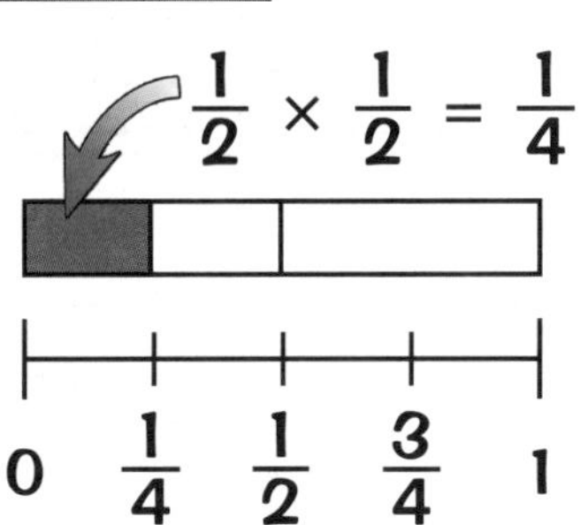

You'll notice the answer's smaller, even though you're multiplying.

Imagine half a cake being cut in half — you get a quarter of a cake.

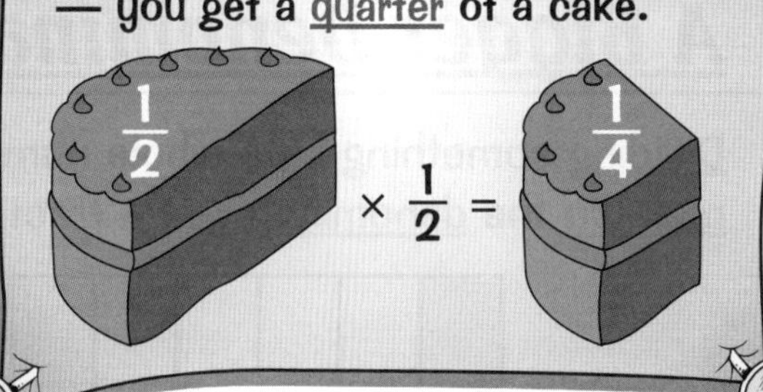

MORE EXAMPLES:

$\frac{1}{2} \times \frac{1}{4} = \frac{1}{8}$ ($1 \times 1 = 1$, $2 \times 4 = 8$)

$\frac{1}{2} \times \frac{3}{4} = \frac{3}{8}$ ($1 \times 3 = 3$, $2 \times 4 = 8$)

$\frac{2}{3} \times \frac{1}{3} = \frac{2}{9}$ ($2 \times 1 = 2$, $3 \times 3 = 9$)

$\frac{2}{3} \times \frac{5}{7} = \frac{10}{21}$ ($2 \times 5 = 10$, $3 \times 7 = 21$)

EVEN MORE EXAMPLES:

Remember to simplify if you can.

$\frac{2}{3} \times \frac{3}{4} = \frac{6}{12} = \frac{1}{2}$ ($2 \times 3 = 6$, $3 \times 4 = 12$, $\div 6$)

$\frac{3}{4} \times \frac{4}{5} = \frac{12}{20} = \frac{3}{5}$ ($3 \times 4 = 12$, $4 \times 5 = 20$, $\div 4$)

"I can multiply fractions by other fractions."

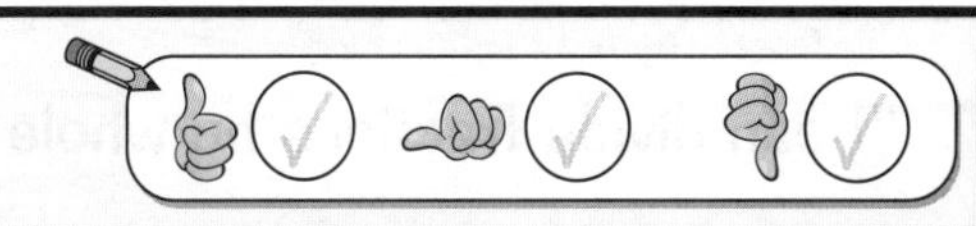

Dividing Fractions by Whole Numbers

Multiply The Denominator

Dividing fractions by whole numbers is easy if you know how.

To divide a fraction by a whole number, multiply the denominator by the whole number.

EXAMPLE:

$\frac{3}{4} \div 2 = \frac{3}{8}$

$4 \times 2 = 8$

To divide a fraction by 2, take the denominator and multiply it by 2

Remember, dividing is the inverse of multiplying. For example, dividing by 2 is the same as multiplying by $\frac{1}{2}$.

$3 \times 1 = 3$

$\frac{3}{4} \times \frac{1}{2} = \frac{3}{8}$

$4 \times 2 = 8$

A Bigger Denominator = a Smaller Fraction

Dividing something by a whole number makes it smaller. That's what happens when you multiply the denominator of a fraction by a whole number — the fraction gets smaller.

$\frac{1}{6} \div 2 = \frac{1}{12}$

$6 \times 2 = 12$

$\frac{2}{5} \div 3 = \frac{2}{15}$

$5 \times 3 = 15$

EXAMPLE:

Rhianna had $\frac{1}{5}$ of a chocolate bar. She divided it into four equal pieces and gave one of them to her sister. What fraction of the chocolate bar did her sister get?

ANSWER: $\frac{1}{5} \div 4 = \frac{1}{20}$

$5 \times 4 = 20$

"I can divide fractions by whole numbers."

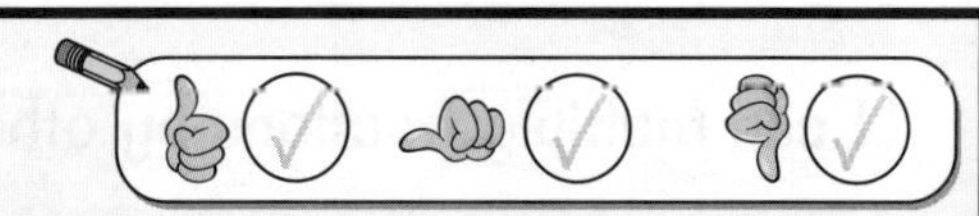

Multiplying or Dividing by 10, 100 or 1000

× by 10, 100 or 1000 — Move the Digits to the Left

To multiply by ten, just move all the digits one place value column to the left. For example, 32.41 × 10 = 324.1. The number gets ten times bigger.

T U t h H T U t

3 2 . 4 1 × 1 0 = 3 2 4 . 1

The 1 moves from hundredths to tenths.
The 4 moves from tenths to units.
The 2 moves from units to tens.
The 3 moves from tens to hundreds.

To multiply by a hundred just move them two places to the left.

T U Th H T U

6 4 × 1 0 0 = 6 4 0 0

You need these 2 zeros to fill the tens and units places. They are called placeholders.

The number gets 100 times bigger.

To multiply by a thousand, move them three places to the left.

÷ by 10, 100 or 1000 — Move the Digits to the Right

To divide by 10, move all the digits 1 place value column to the right. The number gets 10 times smaller.

H T U T U . t

1 6 0 ÷ 1 0 = 1 6 . 0 = 1 6

16.0 = 16 so you don't need to write this zero.

To divide by 100, move everything 2 places to the right. The number gets 100 times smaller.

T U t U . t h th

5 0 . 6 ÷ 1 0 0 = 0 . 5 0 6

You need this zero as a placeholder.

To divide by 1000, move everything 3 places to the right. The number gets 1000 times smaller.

TTh Th H T U T U . t h th

9 7 0 8 0 ÷ 1 0 0 0 = 9 7 . 0 8 0

= 9 7 . 0 8

"I can multiply or divide numbers by 10, 100 or 1000."

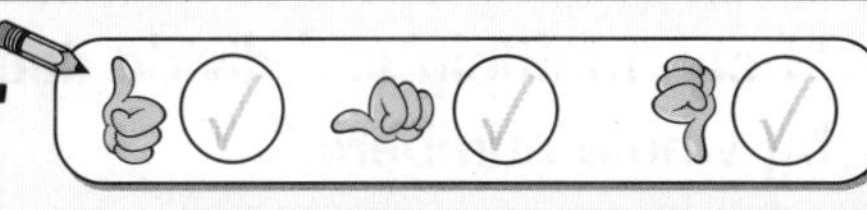

Multiplying and Dividing with Decimals

Ignore The Decimal Point, Then Adjust

To multiply or divide a decimal, do a whole-number calculation first, then adjust.

Multiplying Decimals

EXAMPLE: What is 0.3 × 2?

First do a whole-number calculation, 3 × 2 = 6

BUT 3 is 10 times as big as 0.3. So the answer to 3 × 2 will be 10 times too big. So divide that by 10.

6 ÷ 10 = **0.6**

It's a good idea to estimate before you do the multiplication: 1.92 m × 38 ≈ 2 m × 40 = 80 m

EXAMPLE: What is 1.92 m × 38?

First do a whole-number calculation, 192 × 38

```
     1 9 2
  ×    3 8
  --------
   1 5 3 6
   5 7 6 0
  --------
 = 7 2 9 6
```

BUT 192 is 100 times as big as 1.92. So the answer to 192 × 38 will be 100 times too big. So divide that by 100.

7296 ÷ 100 = **72.96 m**

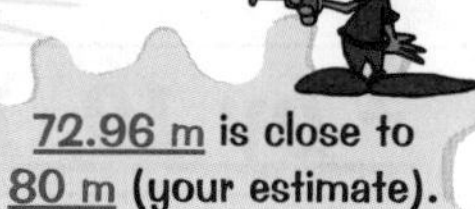

72.96 m is close to 80 m (your estimate).

Dividing Decimals

EXAMPLE: What is 19.2 ÷ 6?

Estimate first: 19.2 ÷ 6 ≈ 18 ÷ 6 = 3

Work out 192 ÷ 6. The answer will be 10 times bigger than 19.2 ÷ 6, so divide it by 10.

192 ÷ 6 → 6) 1 ¹9 ¹2 = 0 3 2 = 32

32 ÷ 10 = 3.2

So 19.2 ÷ 6 = **3.2**

3.2 ≈ 3 (your estimate)

EXAMPLE: What is £32.41 ÷ 7?

Estimate first: £32.41 ÷ 7 ≈ £35 ÷ 7 = £5

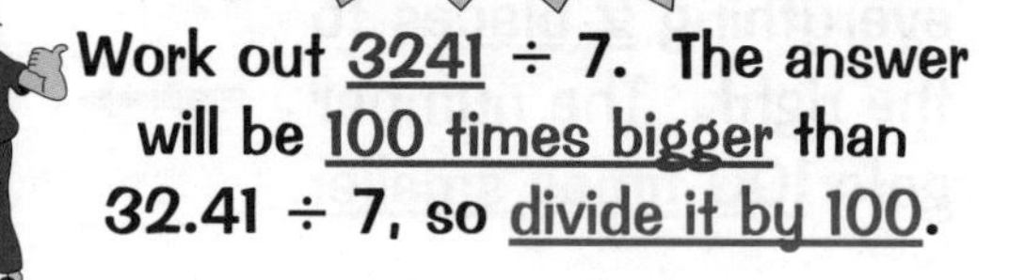

Work out 3241 ÷ 7. The answer will be 100 times bigger than 32.41 ÷ 7, so divide it by 100.

3241 ÷ 7 → 7) 3 ³2 ⁴4 ²1 = 0 4 6 3 = 463

463 ÷ 100 = 4.63

So £32.41 ÷ 7 = **£4.63**

£4.63 ≈ £5

"I can multiply and divide decimal numbers by whole numbers."

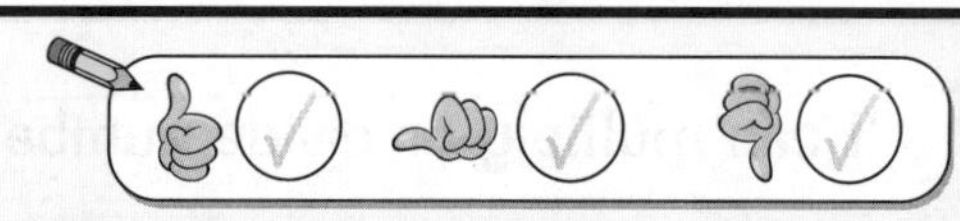

Rounding Decimals

You might have to round DECIMAL NUMBERS to the nearest whole number.
Or, you might have to round them to ONE DECIMAL PLACE (or possibly TWO DECIMAL PLACES). This isn't too bad, but you do have to learn some rules for it:

Rounding to Decimal Places

EXAMPLE: Round 3.635 to 2 decimal places.

1) From the decimal point, mark the number of places you want to keep. → 3 . 6 3 5 (2 decimal places)

2) Look at the next digit to the right. This is the 'DECIDER'.

3) If the DECIDER is 5 or more, then ROUND UP. → Increase the last remaining digit by 1.
If the DECIDER is 4 or less, then ROUND DOWN. → Leave the last remaining digit as it is.
GET RID of the DECIDER and any digits after it.

In 3.635 the DECIDER is 5.
So the last remaining digit, 3, rounds up to 4. The answer is **3.64**

Check How Many Decimal Places You've Got

There must be NO MORE DIGITS after the decimal place you've rounded to (not even zeros).

EXAMPLES: 5.1 rounded to the nearest whole number is 5.
2.371 rounded to 1 decimal place is 2.4
3.843 rounded to 2 decimal places is 3.84

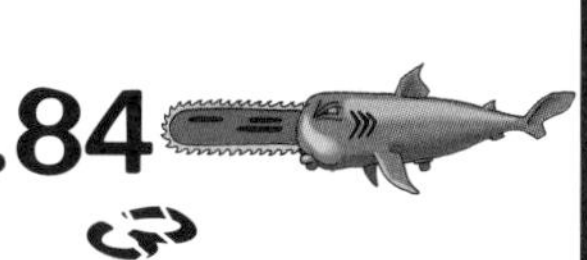

ANOTHER EXAMPLE: What is 62.04 to 1 decimal place?

The decider is 4, so you round down to 62.0
Because you're rounding to 1 decimal place, you have to include the 0. Just putting "62" as your answer would be wrong, as that's rounded to the nearest whole number.

"I can round decimal numbers to a given number of decimal places."

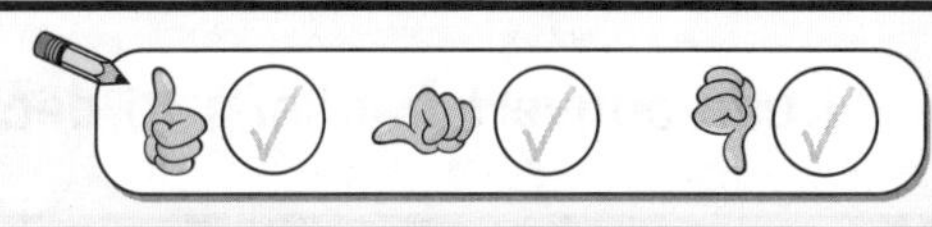

Converting Fractions to Decimals

You can convert any fraction to a decimal.

Find an Equivalent in Tenths or Hundredths or Thousandths...

If the denominator is a factor of 10, 100 or 1000, first find an equivalent fraction in tenths, hundredths or thousandths.
Then, because $\frac{1}{10} = 0.1$, $\frac{1}{100} = 0.01$ and $\frac{1}{1000} = 0.001$,
you know that, for example, $\frac{8}{10} = 0.8$, $\frac{6}{100} = 0.06$, and $\frac{12}{1000} = 0.012$.

EXAMPLES: a) $\frac{2}{5} = \frac{4}{10} = 0.4$ b) $\frac{20}{250} = \frac{80}{1000} = 0.08$

...Or Do The Division

To convert any fraction to a decimal, divide the numerator by the denominator.
That's all a fraction really is: $\frac{1}{2} = 1 \div 2 = 0.5$, $\frac{1}{4} = 1 \div 4 = 0.25$, and so on.

When you see this line you can say "divided by": $\frac{\text{a number}}{\text{another number}}$ = a number divided by another number

EXAMPLE: Convert $\frac{3}{8}$ to a decimal.

The calculation you have to do is $3 \div 8$.

$\frac{3}{8}$ of a pizza is what each person gets if 3 pizzas are divided between 8 people.

An easier calculation is $3000 \div 8$. The answer to that will be 1000 times too big, so divide it by 1000:

$3000 \div 8 \rightarrow$ $8\overline{)3\,{}^{3}0\,{}^{6}0\,{}^{4}0}$ = 0375 = 375

$\rightarrow 375 \div 1000 = 0.375$

Answer: $\frac{3}{8} = 3 \div 8 = \underline{0.375}$

$\frac{3}{8} = 3 \div 8$:

$\frac{3}{8}$

0 0.375 1 2 3

$3 \div 8$

"I can convert fractions to decimals by dividing."

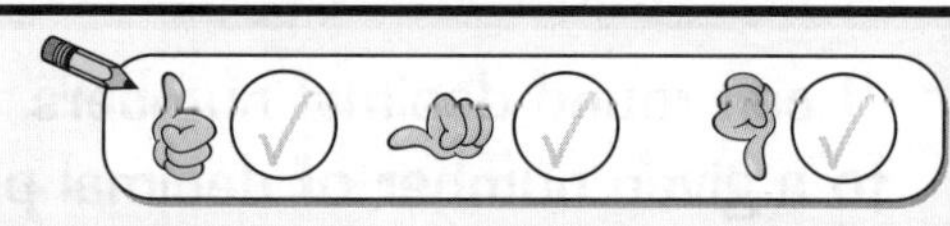

Fractions, Decimals and Percentages

Useful Fractions, Decimals and Percentages...

Learn these common fractions and their EQUIVALENT decimals and percentages:

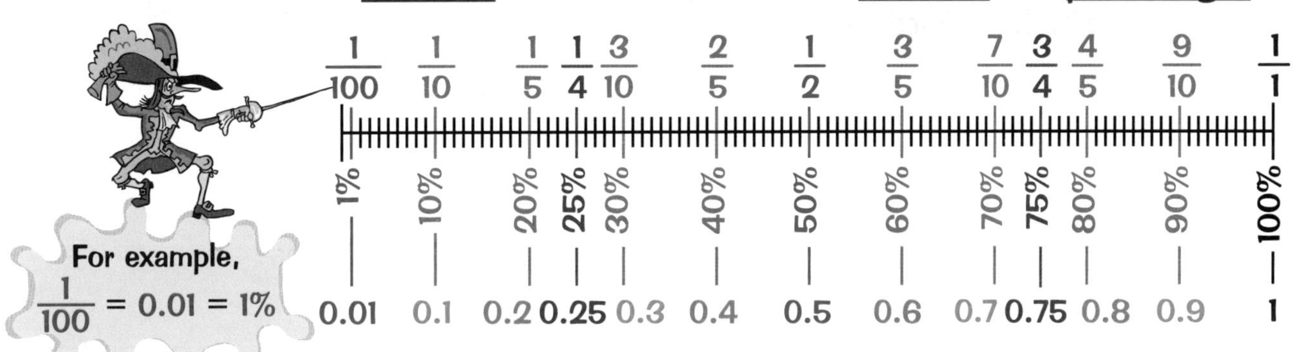

For example, $\frac{1}{100} = 0.01 = 1\%$

...and How To Convert Between Them

Fraction → Percentage: Make an equivalent fraction with a denominator of 100. The numerator is the percentage. $\frac{3}{4} = \frac{75}{100} = 75\%$

Percentage → Fraction: Put the percentage on top and 100 on the bottom, then simplify if you can. $75\% = \frac{75}{100} = \frac{3}{4}$

Decimal → Fraction: Look at the decimal places to see if the denominator will be 10ths, 100ths or 1000ths. Then put the decimal places as the numerator. Simplify if you need to. $0.75 = \frac{75}{100} = \frac{3}{4}$

Fraction → Decimal: Do the division. $\frac{3}{4} = 3 \div 4 = 0.75$

Percentage → Decimal: Divide the percentage by 100. $75\% = 75 \div 100 = 0.75$

Decimal → Percentage: Multiply the decimal by 100. $0.75 \times 100 = 75\%$

EXAMPLES:

a) What is 0.4 as a fraction? $0.4 = \frac{4}{10} = \frac{2}{5}$ (1 decimal place = tenths)

b) Show the recurring decimal 0.666666... as a percentage.

Round to 3 decimal places to get a shorter decimal. The decider is 6, so round up → 0.667

Then, multiply 0.667 by 100: $0.667 \times 100 = 66.7\%$

c) What is $\frac{8}{25}$ as a percentage? $\frac{8}{25} = \frac{32}{100} = 32\%$

"I can convert between fractions, decimals and percentages."

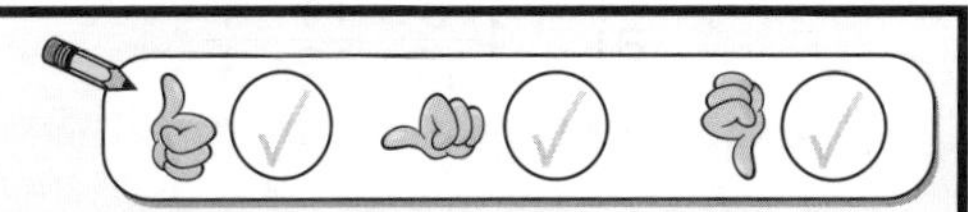

Practice Questions

Start off with the **green** questions — they're the easiest ones.
The **blue** ones are a bit harder, and the **pink** ones are the hardest.

1 Simplify these fractions.

a) $\frac{4}{8}$ b) $\frac{18}{24}$ c) $\frac{10}{25}$

2 Convert these fractions so that they have the same denominator.

a) $\frac{1}{2}$ and $\frac{2}{3}$ b) $\frac{1}{3}$ and $\frac{3}{4}$ c) $\frac{7}{8}$ and $\frac{1}{6}$

3 Solve these fraction calculations:

a) $\frac{1}{12} + \frac{5}{6}$ b) $\frac{3}{7} \times \frac{2}{5}$ c) $\frac{4}{9} + \frac{1}{6}$

4 Round these numbers to 2 decimal places.

a) 69.508 b) 1.265 c) 19.998

5 Divide these fractions by 6.

a) $\frac{1}{3}$ b) $\frac{4}{5}$ c) $\frac{3}{11}$

6 Put the following fractions in order from smallest to largest:

a) $\frac{2}{3}, \frac{3}{4}, \frac{7}{12}, \frac{1}{2}$ b) $\frac{5}{12}, \frac{1}{5}, \frac{2}{6}, \frac{3}{10}$ c) $\frac{2}{9}, \frac{1}{6}, \frac{1}{3}, \frac{7}{18}$

7 Solve these decimal calculations. Round your answers to 1 decimal place.

a) 12.46 × 1000 b) 419.2 ÷ 100 c) 10 × 85.705

8 Put the following fractions in order from smallest to largest:

a) $1\frac{5}{12}, \frac{14}{12}, \frac{4}{3}$ b) $2\frac{1}{5}, 2\frac{2}{3}, \frac{37}{15}$ c) $3\frac{1}{3}, \frac{13}{4}, \frac{7}{2}$

Practice Questions

9 Solve these fraction calculations:

a) $2\frac{1}{4} - 1\frac{3}{4}$ b) $1\frac{1}{3} + 3\frac{1}{2}$ c) $\frac{5}{9} \times \frac{2}{5}$

10 Multiply these by 5:

a) 5.84 b) 9.7 cm c) £8.22

11 Divide these numbers by 3:

a) 6.3 b) 12.06 c) 34.89

12 Convert these fractions to decimals:

a) $\frac{3}{5}$ b) $\frac{7}{20}$ c) $\frac{7}{8}$

13 Convert these fractions to percentages.

a) $\frac{12}{50}$ b) $\frac{2}{10}$ c) $\frac{3}{8}$

14 Adnan, Ben and Cat each have the same number of sweets.

Adnan eats 0.61 of his sweets, Ben eats 58.5% of his sweets and Cat eats $\frac{6}{10}$ of her sweets.

a) Who has the most sweets left?

b) Who has the fewest sweets left?

15 Danny has two part-eaten pies. One has $\frac{3}{4}$ left. The other has $\frac{1}{5}$ left.

a) What total fraction of one pie does he have left?

b) What is this fraction as a decimal?

c) Does he have enough left to give 5 people 0.17 of a pie each?

Relative Sizes

Scaling up and down is all about multiplying and dividing.

"Scaling up by a factor of five" just means multiplying by 5.

"Scaling down by a factor of five" just means dividing by 5.

You Can Show Scaling Using Number Lines

EXAMPLE: 16 is four times as many as 4.
What number is four times as many as 12?

Draw 2 number lines — one counting up in ones, and one scaled up by four.

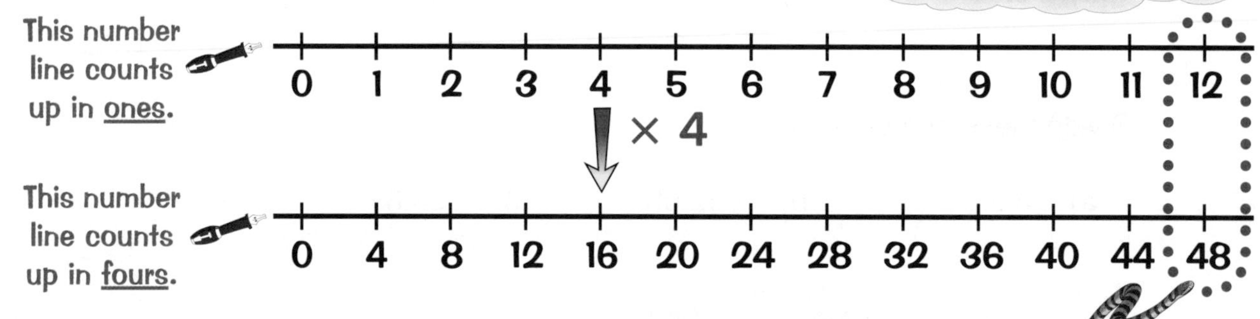

Each number on the top number line lines up with one four times as big on the bottom number line.

Find 12 on the top number line. It lines up with 48 on the bottom number line. So the answer is 48.

Use Scaling to Solve Money Problems

EXAMPLE: One jar of sprout spread costs 14p. How much will six jars cost?

So, six jars of sprout spread cost 84p.

ANOTHER EXAMPLE: In a different shop you can buy eight jars of sprout spread for 96p. How much will three jars cost?

First you need to divide by 8 to find out how much 1 jar costs: 96p ÷ 8 = 12p

Then you need to multiply by 3 to find the cost of 3 jars: 12p × 3 = 36p

So, three jars of sprout spread cost 36p.

"I can solve problems that are to do with the relative sizes of two amounts."

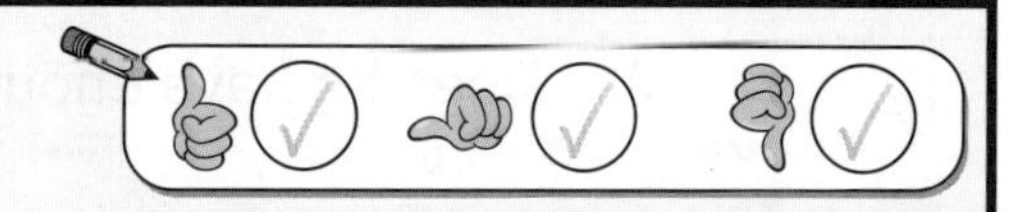

Relative Sizes

Ratios Compare One Part to Another Part

Look at this pattern:

For the 2 white stars there are 6 blue stars.
So for every white star there are 3 blue stars.
The ratio is 1 white to 3 blue. You can also write 1:3.

You can use ratios to solve problems.

EXAMPLE: Crazy Jack is offering 1 free shark with every 6 toothbrushes bought. I buy 18 toothbrushes. How many free sharks will I get?

The ratio is 6 toothbrushes to 1 shark (6:1).
18 toothbrushes is 3 lots of 6 toothbrushes.

6 toothbrushes get... 1 shark
×3 ×3
18 toothbrushes get... ? sharks

So I get 3 lots of 1 free shark.
$3 \times 1 =$ 3 free sharks.

Proportions Compare a Part to the Whole Thing

Look again at the pattern at the top of the page. You can describe it in another way... "In every 4 stars there are 3 blue stars and 1 white star." The proportion of blue stars is 3 in every 4. The proportion of white stars is 1 in every 4.

Proportions are really another way of writing fractions.
The proportion "1 in every 4" is the same as the fraction $\frac{1}{4}$.

EXAMPLE: In my herd of zebras, 2 in every 9 zebras are orange. There are 36 zebras in my herd. How many are orange?

There are 2 orange zebras in every 9, so we need to know how many 9s there are in 36: $36 \div 9 = 4$.
So there are 4 lots of 9 zebras in the herd.
So there must be 4 lots of 2 orange zebras.
$2 \times 4 =$ 8 orange zebras.

You can use proportions in recipes...

EXAMPLE: A recipe for 2 people uses 3 daffodils and 2 eggs.

a) Gary puts 6 eggs in. How many daffodils does he need?
6 eggs is 3 times as many eggs as in the recipe.
So he needs 3 times as many daffodils too. $3 \times 3 =$ 9 daffodils.

b) How many eggs and daffodils would he need for 8 people?
He needs 4 times as many ingredients for 8 people as he does for 2.
So he will need $3 \times 4 =$ 12 daffodils and $2 \times 4 =$ 8 eggs.

"I can solve problems that are to do with the relative sizes of two amounts."

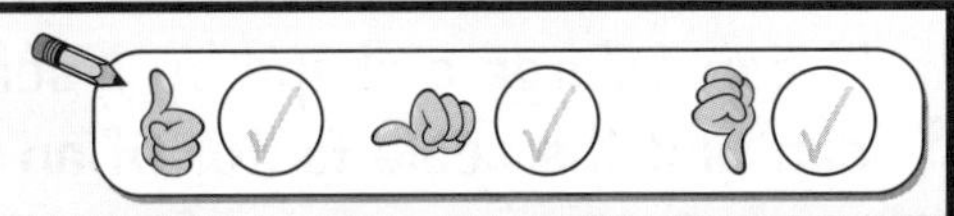

Scale Factors

Shapes can be Scaled Up or Down

Enlargements make a shape get bigger — how much bigger depends on the scale factor. Every side of the shape is multiplied by the scale factor.

EXAMPLE: Enlarge shape K below by a scale factor of 2.

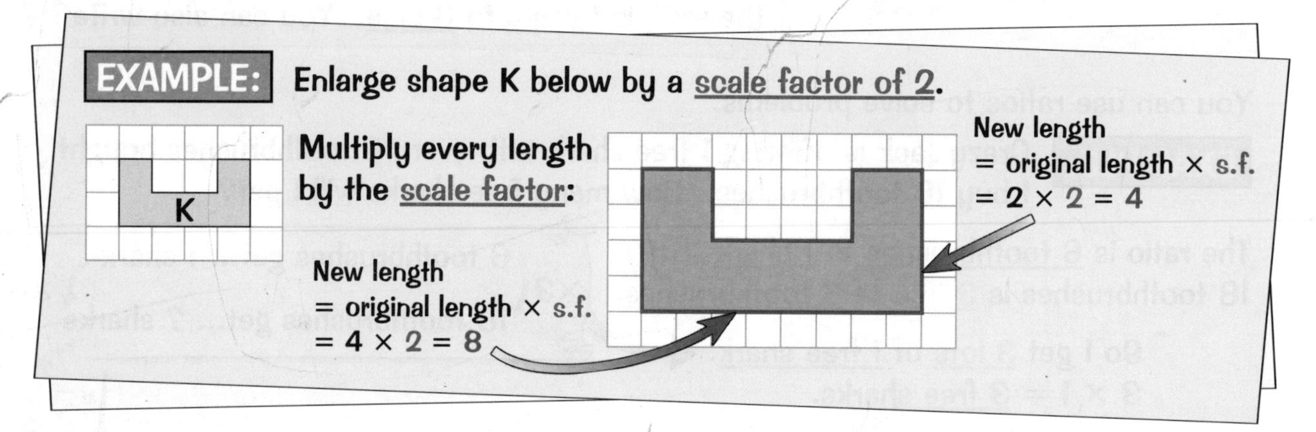

EXAMPLE: A shape has been enlarged by a scale factor of 5. If the shortest side on the enlarged shape is 15 cm long, how long is the shortest side on the original shape?

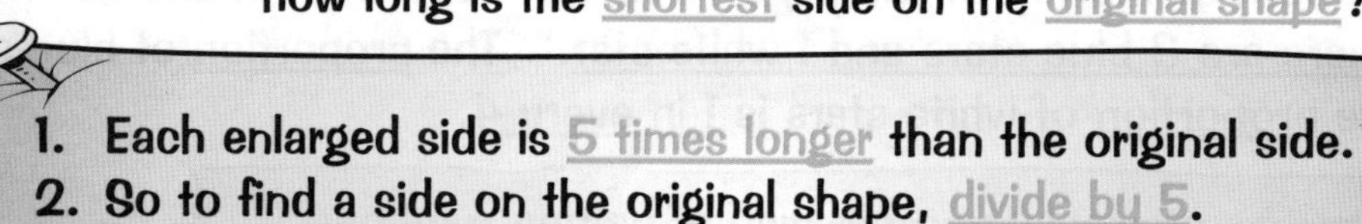

1. Each enlarged side is 5 times longer than the original side.
2. So to find a side on the original shape, divide by 5.
3. The shortest side on the original shape is 15 ÷ 5 = 3 cm long.

Find the Scale Factor by Dividing

You can work out the scale factor by dividing a length on the enlarged shape by the length of the same side on the original shape.

EXAMPLE: Shape B is an enlargement of shape A. Using the lengths given, work out the scale factor of the enlargement.

Base of shape B = 21 cm
Base of shape A = 7 cm
To find the scale factor, divide the enlarged length by the original length: scale factor = 21 ÷ 7 = 3.

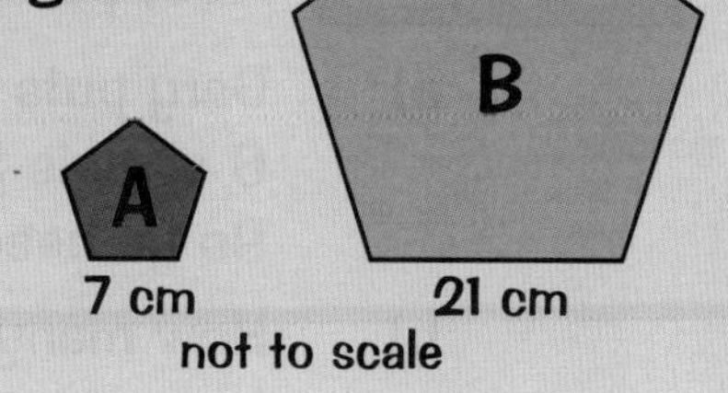

"I can enlarge a shape by a scale factor and I can find the scale factor of an enlarged shape."

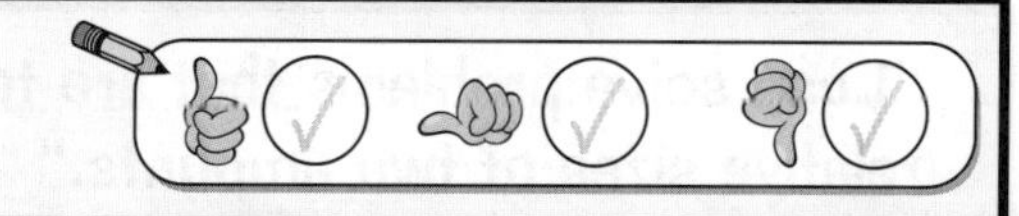

Percentages of Amounts

Finding Percentages of Amounts

Finding a percentage of an amount isn't too bad.
That's because...

$10\% = \frac{10}{100} = \frac{1}{10}$ ...and to find a tenth of something, you just divide by 10.

So to find 10% of something, just divide it by 10.

EXAMPLE: What is 10% of £420?

ANSWER: 10% of 420 = 420 ÷ 10 = £42

Finding 50% is easy too. 50% is just a half. For example, 50% of 70 kg is 70 ÷ 2 = 35 kg.

If you can find 10%, it's easy to find 20% or 30%.
(Just find 10% then multiply it by 2 or 3...)

You can also use 10% to find 5% or 15%.

EXAMPLE: Jim is about to eat a 120 g burger. 15% of the burger's mass is cabbage. How many grams of cabbage are there in his burger?

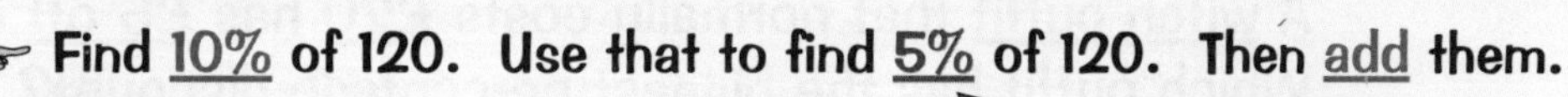

Find 10% of 120. Use that to find 5% of 120. Then add them.

10% of 120 g = 120 g ÷ 10
= 12 g

5% is just half of 10%

5% of 120 g = 12 g ÷ 2
= 6 g

So there are 12 + 6 = 18 g of cabbage in Jim's burger.

EXAMPLE: Peter eats 35% of a circle of cheese.
How many degrees of the cheese circle has he eaten?

There are 360° in a circle.

1. Find 10% of 360°. → 10% of 360° = 360° ÷ 10
= 36°
2. Use that to find 30% and 5% of 360°.

30% of 360° = 36° × 3
= 108°

5% of 360° = 36° ÷ 2
= 18°

3. Then add them: 108° + 18° = 126°

So 35% of 360° = 126°

"I can find a percentage of an amount."

Comparing Using Percentages

Writing a Number as a Percentage of Another

To write one number as a percentage of another number write it as a fraction and then convert to a percentage.

EXAMPLE: There are 15 girls and 10 boys in Mario's class. What percentage of the class are girls?

First write the total amount as the denominator of the fraction. $15 + 10 = 25 \rightarrow \frac{}{25}$

Then write the number of girls as the numerator.

Convert the fraction into a percentage.

$$\frac{15}{25} \overset{\times 4}{=} \frac{60}{100} = 60\%$$

Use Percentages to Compare Amounts

You can compare amounts by converting them into percentages.

EXAMPLE: A superhero outfit that normally costs £50 has £10 off in a sale. A witch outfit that normally costs £20 has £5 off in the sale. Which outfit has the biggest percentage discount?

You need to find the money off each outfit as a percentage of the total price.

Put the money off as the numerator.

Put the total price as the denominator.

superhero outfit: $\frac{10}{50} \overset{\times 2}{=} \frac{20}{100} = 20\%$

witch outfit: $\frac{5}{20} \overset{\times 5}{=} \frac{25}{100} = 25\%$

So the witch outfit has the biggest percentage discount.

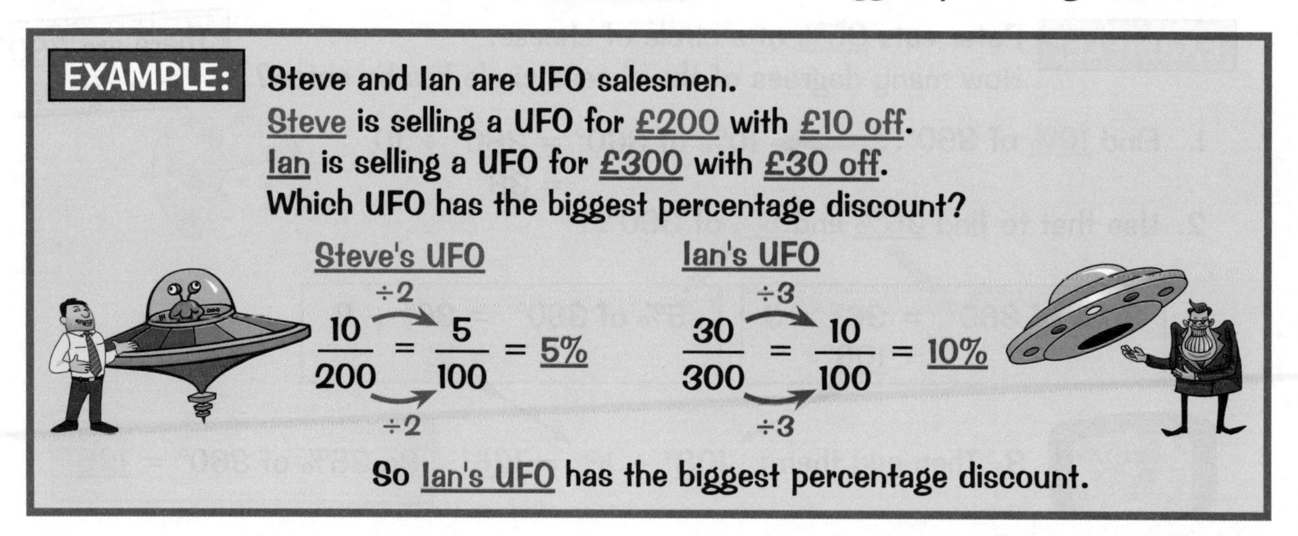

EXAMPLE: Steve and Ian are UFO salesmen.
Steve is selling a UFO for £200 with £10 off.
Ian is selling a UFO for £300 with £30 off.
Which UFO has the biggest percentage discount?

Steve's UFO: $\frac{10}{200} \overset{\div 2}{=} \frac{5}{100} = 5\%$

Ian's UFO: $\frac{30}{300} \overset{\div 3}{=} \frac{10}{100} = 10\%$

So Ian's UFO has the biggest percentage discount.

"I can use percentages to compare amounts."

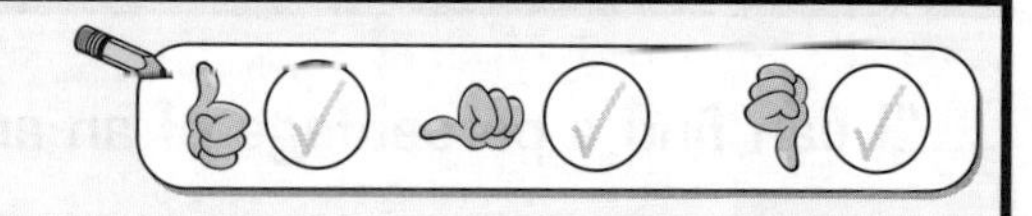

Unequal Sharing

Sometimes Things are Shared Unequally

EXAMPLE: Matt eats 2 slices of pizza for every 1 that Nic eats.

Another way to say this is:
'They share the pizza in the ratio 2:1'.

Nic's share

Matt's share

This means that:
There are 3 shares of pizza in total.
For every 1 share that Nic gets, Matt gets 2 shares.

So Nic has $\frac{1}{3}$ of the total number of slices and Matt has $\frac{2}{3}$ of the total number.

If Nic has 4 slices of pizza, Matt has twice as many, so he has 8 slices.
If Matt has 18 slices of pizza, Nic has half that amount, so she has 9 slices.

EXAMPLE: Rob and Richard are elephant cleaners.
Rob cleans faster than Richard, so they decide that for every £5 they earn, Rob gets £4 and Richard gets £1.

Another way to say this is:
'They share the money in the ratio 4:1'.

This means that:
There are 5 shares of money in total.
For every 1 share that Richard gets, Rob gets 4 shares.

So Richard has $\frac{1}{5}$ of the total money and Rob has $\frac{4}{5}$ of the total amount.

If Richard earns £20, Rob earns four times more, so he has £80.
If Rob earns £40, Richard earns four times less, so he earns £10.

EXAMPLE: Troy shares 600 grapes with his brother Tim, in the ratio 7:5.

This means that: There are 12 shares of grapes in total.
For every 7 shares Troy gets, Tim gets 5 shares.

Next: Divide the 600 grapes by 12 to find how much it is for ONE SHARE
then multiply by 7 to find how much 7 SHARES ARE
and multiply by 5 to find how much 5 SHARES ARE.

So... $600 \div 12 = 50$ (for 1 share)
$50 \times 7 = 350$ (for 7 shares)
and $50 \times 5 = 250$ (for 5 shares)
So 600 grapes split in the ratio 7:5 is 350:250

You can check this is right by adding the amounts:
$350 + 250 = 600$

"I can work out how to share things unequally."

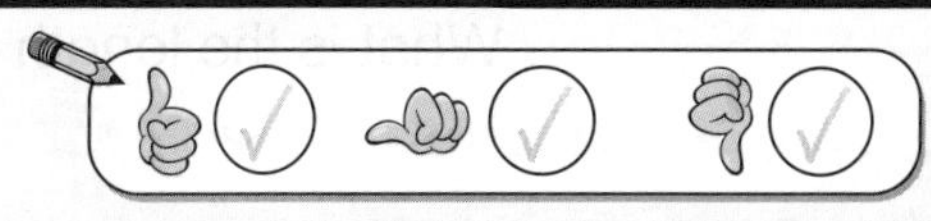

Practice Questions

Start off with the **green** questions — they're the easiest ones.
The **blue** ones are a bit harder, and the **pink** ones are the hardest.

1 Seven jars of rhubarb cost 84p. How much will one jar cost?

2 20 is five times as many as 4. What number is five times as many as 13?

3 Sarah buys 80 hairbands. 20% of the hairbands are blue.

How many blue hairbands did she buy?

4 A recipe for 2 people uses 1 lemon and 4 eggs.

a) Mavis uses 12 eggs. How many lemons will she need?

b) How many lemons and eggs are needed for 20 people?

5 Elisa gets two free keyrings with every 8 chocolate bars she buys.

She buys 24 chocolate bars. How many free keyrings will she get?

6 Mitch buys 28 cans of paint. 2 in every 7 cans are pink.

How many cans of Mitch's paint are pink?

7 Copy the shape to the right onto a large grid.

a) Enlarge this shape by a scale factor of 2.

b) The same shape is enlarged by a scale factor of 6.
What is the length of the top of the enlarged shape?

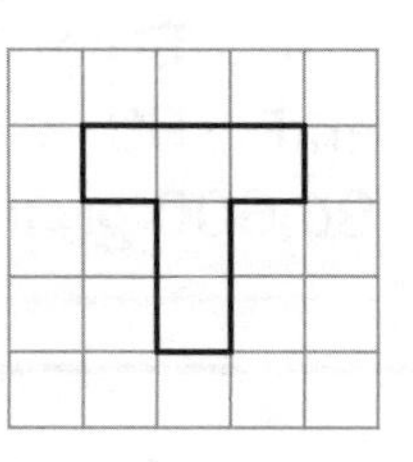

Practice Questions

8 Shape W is an enlargement of shape V.
The longest side of shape V measures 7 cm
and the longest side of shape W measures 70 cm.

What is the scale factor of the enlargement?

9 Gina has made 240 biscuits.
65% of the biscuits are orange flavoured. The rest are chocolate.

How many orange flavoured biscuits has Gina made?

10 There are 360° in a circle. George eats 55% of a pie.
How many degrees of the pie has he eaten?

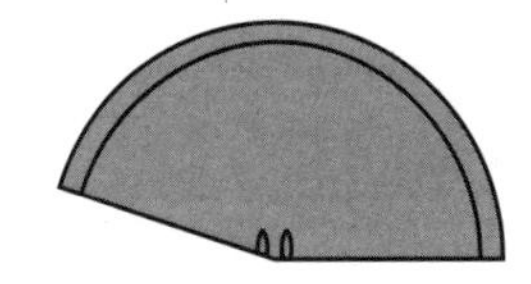

Not drawn to scale.

11 Penny and Luc have found a treasure chest in the garden.
The chest contains 150 gold coins. Penny and Luc share
the coins between them in the ratio 2:1.

How many gold coins do they each get?

12 Charlie is selling ice cream for £3.00 plus an extra 75p off.
Johnny is selling ice cream for £2.00 plus an extra 40p off.
Who is giving the biggest percentage discount?

13 Hati and Dom have a bag of raisins. They share the raisins in the ratio 3:2.
Hati gets the bigger share. If Hati eats 15 raisins, how many does Dom eat?

Sequences

You can Find a Rule for the Next Term

Look at this number sequence: 2, 5, 8, 11, 14, 17...

The rule is: Add on 3 to get from one term to the next.

EXAMPLE: A number sequence goes 5, 11, 17, 23...
What is the rule to get from one term to the next?

To find the rule, find the difference between each term.
So 11 – 5 = 6

So the rule is: Add on 6 to get from one term to the next.

You can use rules like the one above to generate number sequences.

Follow the Rule to Continue a Sequence

Every sequence follows a rule. You can use it to write the next terms.

EXAMPLES: a) Write the next three terms in the sequence 3, 7, 11, 15...

3 → 7 → 11 → 15
+4 +4 +4

The rule is: Add on 4 to the previous number.

So the next three terms are:
15 + 4 = 19
19 + 4 = 23
23 + 4 = 27

b) Write the next three terms in the sequence 21, 19, 17, 15...

The rule is: Take 2 off the previous number.

So the next three terms are:
15 – 2 = 13
13 – 2 = 11
11 – 2 = 9

"I can generate and describe number sequences."

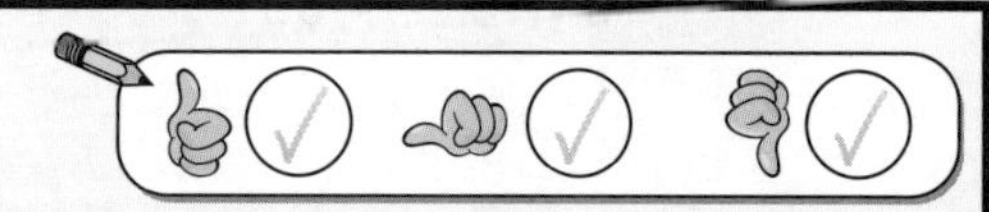

Missing Number Problems

Symbols Can Stand For Missing Numbers

You can use a symbol to stand in for a number you don't know.

EXAMPLE: Mick says, "If I double my age and add five I get the answer 203. How old am I?"

ANSWER: $\triangle$ = Mick's age.

Remember to say what your symbol stands for.

Mick doubled his age, then added 5 to get 203.
So work backwards:
203 – 5 must be double Mick's age.

$203 - 5 = 198$

$2 \times \triangle = 198$

So $\triangle = 198 \div 2 = 99$

$\triangle$ is being multiplied by 2, so divide both sides by 2 to get $\triangle$ on its own.

Letters Are Often Used Instead Of Symbols

You can also use a letter to stand for a number that you don't know.
It's quicker and easier than drawing a symbol every time.

If y is the unknown number then:

$y + 3$ means you are adding 3 to it.
$y - 2$ means you are subtracting 2 from it.
$4y$ means you are multiplying it by 4 ($4 \times y$).

EXAMPLE: James has 27 apples. James has 3 times more than Katie. How many apples does Katie have?

The number of apples Katie has is unknown. Call this y apples.
James has 27 apples, which is $3 \times y$ (3 times more than Katie).

So $3y = 27$

Divide both sides by 3 to get y on its own.

$y = 27 \div 3 = 9$
So Katie has 9 apples.

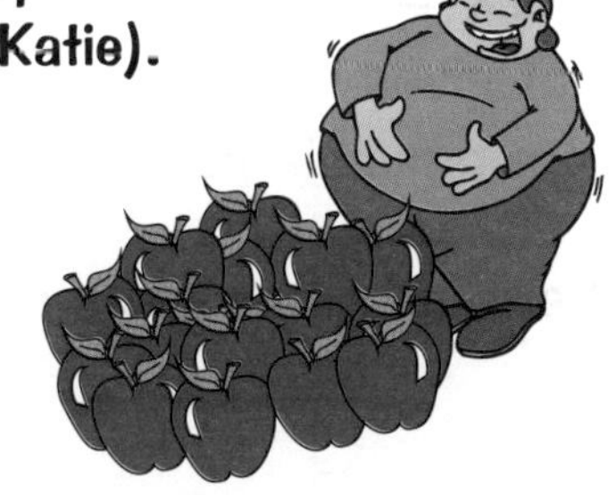

"I can solve missing number problems using symbols and letters."

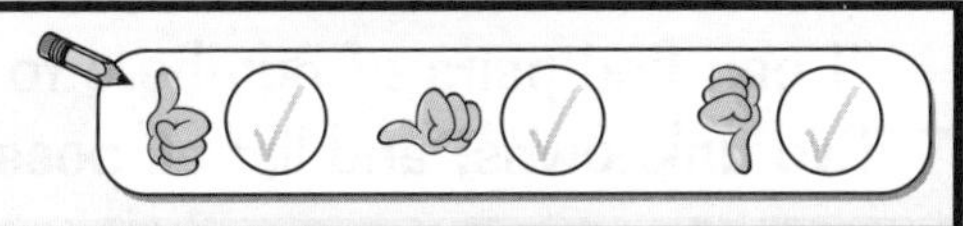

Two Missing Numbers

Problems Can Have Two Missing Numbers

EXAMPLE: Dave is told that $A \times B = 18$, where A and B are whole numbers. Write down 3 possible pairs of values for A and B.

Try different numbers for A, and work out what B would need to be to give 18.

Try $A = 1$. $1 \times 18 = 18$, so $B = 18$.
Try $A = 2$. $2 \times 9 = 18$, so $B = 9$.
Try $A = 3$. $3 \times 6 = 18$, so $B = 6$. That's 3 possible pairs, so stop there.

EXAMPLE: Here are 5 number cards.
X, Y and Z each stand for different whole numbers.

The sum of all the cards is 20.
If $Z = 5$, write down a possible pair of values for X and Y.

ANSWER: You can simplify the question above...

$X + X + Y + 5 + 5 = 20$
$X + X + Y + 10 = 20$
So $X + X + Y = 10$
$2X + Y = 10$

You know that $Z = 5$ so you can put that straight in.

Take away the value of Z from both sides so that you're just left with what X and Y are worth.

Now try substituting in numbers for X and Y to make 10.

Substitute is just a fancy word for swap.

Try $X = 1$
So $2X = 2 \times 1 = 2$
That gives you $2 + Y = 10$, so $Y = 8$
So a possible pair of values would be $X = 1$ and $Y = 8$.

There are other pairs of answers too: $X = 2$ $Y = 6$
$X = 3$ $Y = 4$
$X = 4$ $Y = 2$

"I can find pairs of numbers to solve problems with two unknowns, and list all possible combinations."

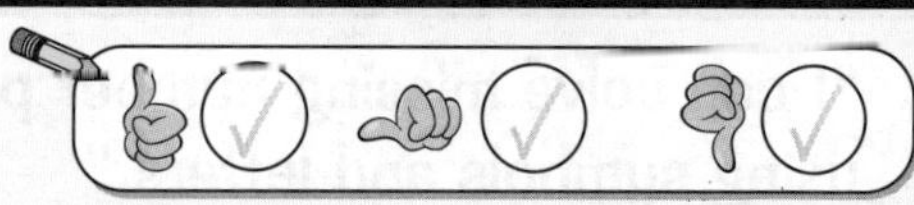

Formulas

A Formula is Used to Work Out an Amount

A formula tells you how to work out one quantity when you know a different quantity.

This formula is for working out how many legs a group of ants has altogether:

legs = 6 × number of ants

EXAMPLE: How many legs do 7 ants have altogether?
Substitute 7 into the formula for the number of ants:

legs = 6 × number of ants
= 6 × 7
= 42 legs altogether

Here's a harder example:

EXAMPLE: The formula for the area of a trapezium is:

$$\text{Area} = \frac{1}{2}(\text{top} + \text{base}) \times \text{height}$$

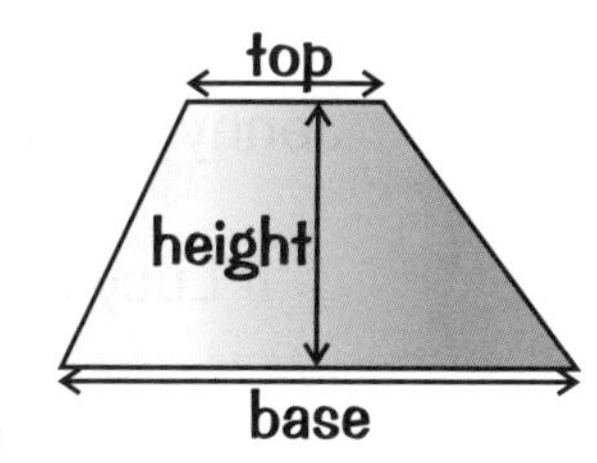

Find the area of a trapezium where the top = 2 cm, the base = 4 cm, and the height = 3 cm.

1) Write out the formula.
2) Write it again underneath but with numbers in place of the words.
3) Work it out in stages.

$\text{Area} = \frac{1}{2}(\text{top} + \text{base}) \times \text{height}$

$\text{Area} = \frac{1}{2}(2 + 4) \times 3$

Use BODMAS — so work out the brackets first.

$\text{Area} = \frac{1}{2} \times 6 \times 3$

$\text{Area} = 3 \times 3$

$\text{Area} = 9 \text{ cm}^2$

Don't forget — the answer might need a unit of measurement.

You Can Write Your Own Formula

This isn't as hard as it sounds. Just think about what you'd do if it were all numbers.

EXAMPLE: Hedgehog-flavoured crisps cost 35p a bag.
Write a formula so that you can calculate the total cost of buying any number of bags.

Put what you want to work out at the beginning before the "=" sign.

Total Cost = Number of bags × 35p

"I can use formulas written in words."

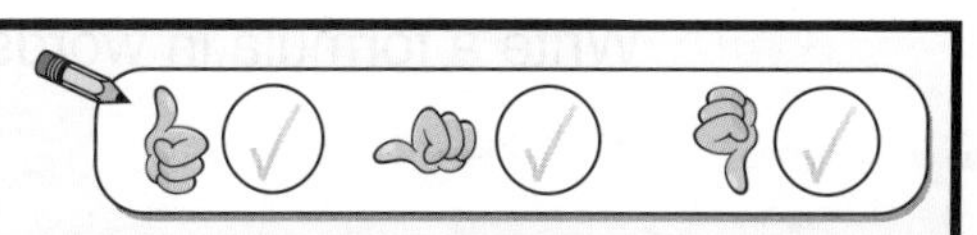

Practice Questions

Start off with the green questions — they're the easiest ones.
The blue ones are a bit harder, and the pink ones are the hardest.

1 A number sequence has the rule "Add 5". The first three terms are 1, 6, 11...

Write down the next three terms.

2 A number sequence goes 5, 9, 13, 17...

a) What is the rule to find the next term?

b) Find the 7th term.

3 Jenny has △ pounds in her purse. Lucy has 4 times more.

If Lucy has 24 pounds, how many does Jenny have?

4 The number of pens in the CGP supply cupboard is given by a formula:
Number of pens = 5 × Number of staff

There are 12 members of staff. How many pens are there in the cupboard?

5 You are told that a + b = 5, and that a and b are whole numbers.

Find a possible pair of numbers for a and b.

6 Antonio opens a cafe. He sells 4 cakes on the first day, 6 on the second day and 8 on the third day.

If the pattern continues, how many will he sell on the 6th day?

7 A farmer has 4 times more cows than chickens.

Write a formula in words for working out the number of cows.

Practice Questions

8 The volume of the shape below is given by the formula:
Volume = ½ × Base × Height × Length

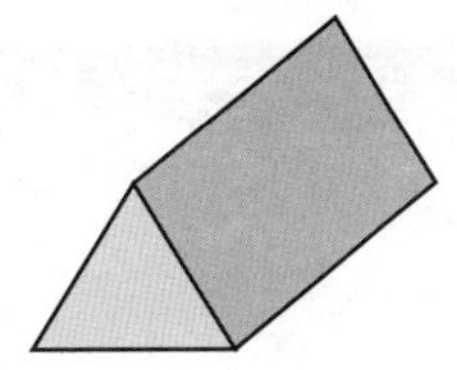

The shape has a base of 4 cm, a height of 3 cm and a length of 4 cm.
What is its volume?

9 John says, "If you triple the number of postcards in my collection, then take away 12, you get 21."

How many postcards does he have?

10 A shop sells 4 bowls and 4 plates for £36.

If each bowl costs £4, how much does one plate cost?

11 Find the missing numbers in this sequence.
The rule is "take ☆".

12 Below are some number cards.
A, B and C represent whole numbers.

The sum of these cards is 14.
If C = 3, write down a possible pair of values for A and B.

Units

Learn these Conversion Factors

You need to know these conversion factors between large and small units.

1 kg = 1000 g

1 cm = 10 mm
1 m = 100 cm
1 km = 1000 m

1 litre = 1000 ml

If you start with small units...
a conversion gives fewer BIGGER units.

To go from small to BIG units, DIVIDE.

If you start with BIG units...
a conversion gives more smaller units.

To go from BIG to small units, MULTIPLY.

Try to remember one example — it'll help you remember the rule. For example, your height in centimetres and in metres. Small unit to big: 154 cm ÷ 100 = 1.54 m

EXAMPLES:

a) Fred's walk to school is 2.75 km. How far is this in metres?

The conversion factor you need is 1 km = 1000 m.

You're going from a big unit to a small one, so MULTIPLY.
2.75 × 1000 = 2750 m

b) Our local shop sells "Froggatt's Mashed Sprout Window Cleaner". One bottle contains 1500 ml. How much is this in litres?

The conversion factor you need is 1 litre = 1000 ml.

You're going from a small unit to a big one, so DIVIDE.
1500 ÷ 1000 = 1.5 l

c) Gary's pet rock has a mass of 563 grams. How much is this in kg?

You'll need to use 1 kg = 1000 g as your conversion factor.

You're going from a small unit to a big one, so DIVIDE.
563 ÷ 1000 = 0.563 kg

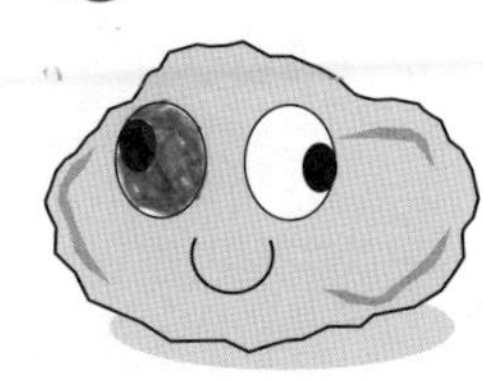

"I can convert between units for measurements of length, mass and volume."

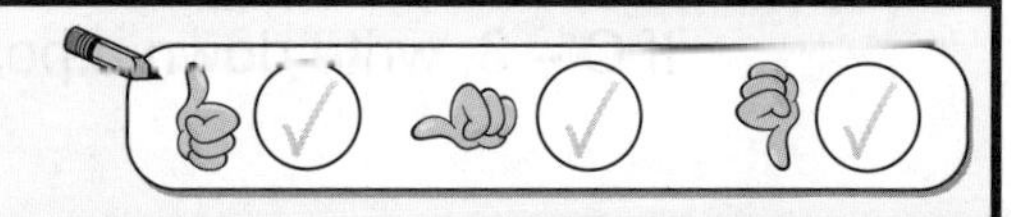

Units

Converting Time May Need More Than One Step

Remember:

1 minute = 60 seconds
1 hour = 60 minutes
1 day = 24 hours
1 week = 7 days
1 year = 365 days

EXAMPLE: Jim books a last-minute holiday to Cumbria. His flight leaves in exactly 1 day. How many minutes is this?

You have to do this in two steps.

First, convert to hours:
1 day = 24 hours

Then convert to minutes:
1 hour = 60 minutes, so 24 × 60 = 1440 mins

$$\begin{array}{r} 60 \\ \times\ 24 \\ \hline 240 \\ 1200 \\ \hline 1440 \end{array}$$

Learn the Mile to Kilometre Conversion

This symbol just means "is approximately equal to".

To convert miles to kilometres, divide by 5 then multiply by 8.
To convert kilometres to miles, divide by 8 then multiply by 5.

EXAMPLES:

a) A car breaks down 48 kilometres before its destination. What is this in miles?

Divide by 8, so 48 ÷ 8 = 6.

Multiply by 5, so 6 × 5 = 30.

So 48 kilometres ≈ 30 miles.

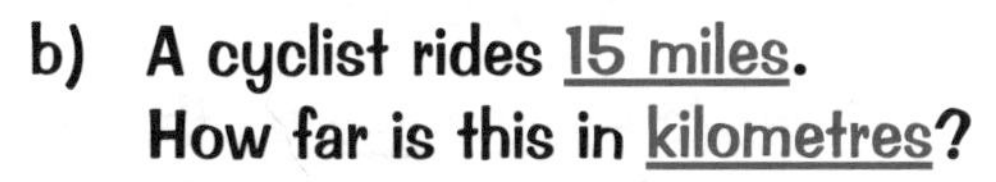

b) A cyclist rides 15 miles. How far is this in kilometres?

Divide by 5, so 15 ÷ 5 = 3.

Multiply by 8, so 3 × 8 = 24.

So 15 miles ≈ 24 kilometres.

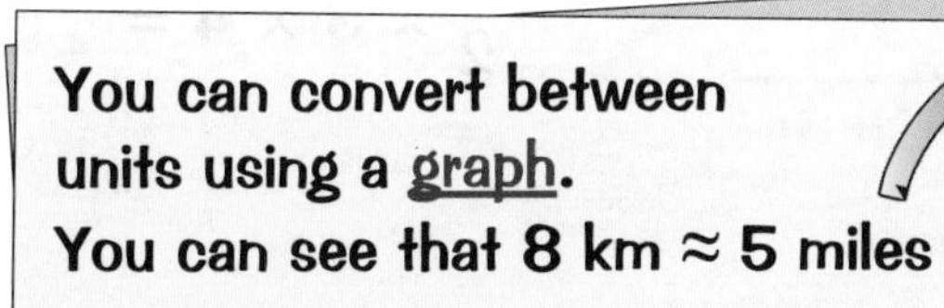

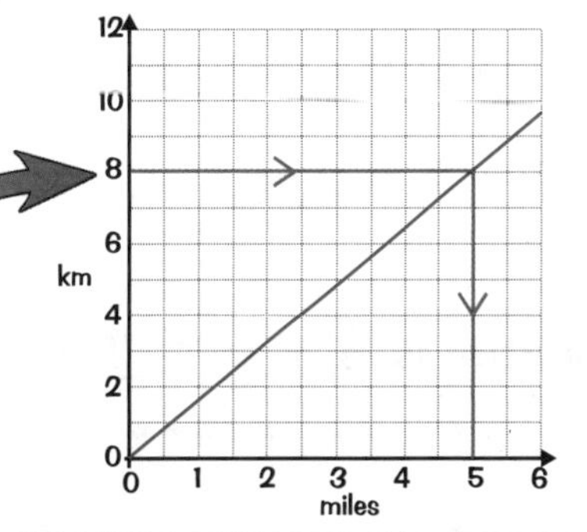

"I can convert between different units of time, and between miles and kilometres."

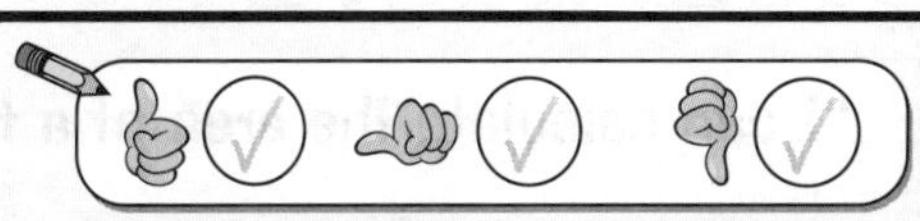

Area of a Triangle

A Triangle is Half a Rectangle

Remember, to find the area of a rectangle you do:

Area = Base × Height

There's a clever way to find the areas of triangles.
A right-angled triangle covers half the area of the rectangle that surrounds it, so...

Area of triangle $= \frac{1}{2} \times$ Base × Height

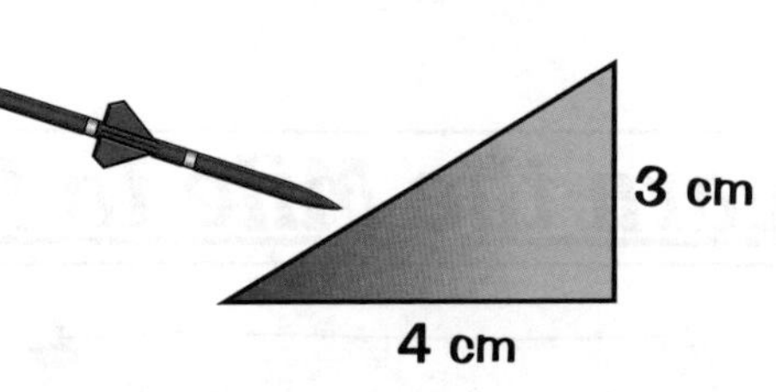

EXAMPLE: Find the area of this triangle.

The base is 4 cm and the height is 3 cm.

Area $= \frac{1}{2} \times 4 \times 3 = \underline{6\ \text{cm}^2}$

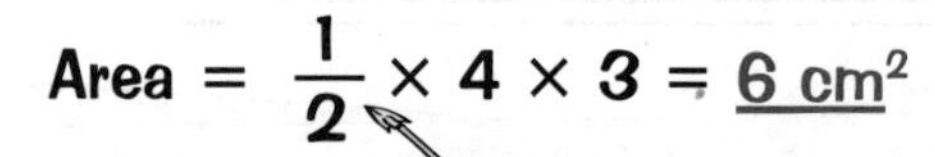

Multiplying a whole number by a fraction is just like finding a fraction of something. So 4 × 3 = 12, and ½ of 12 = 6.

EXAMPLE: Work out the area of this beautifully shaded shape.

Split it up into simple shapes:

1) There's a rectangle on the left.
Its height is 3 cm and its base is 2 cm.

2) There's a triangle on the right.
Its height is 3 cm and its base is 6 – 2 = 4 cm.

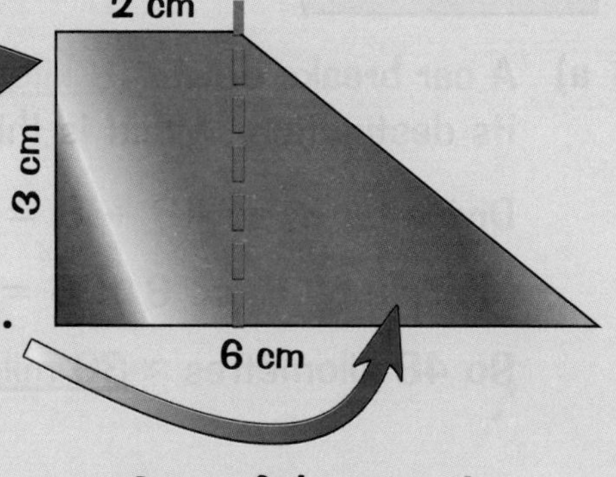

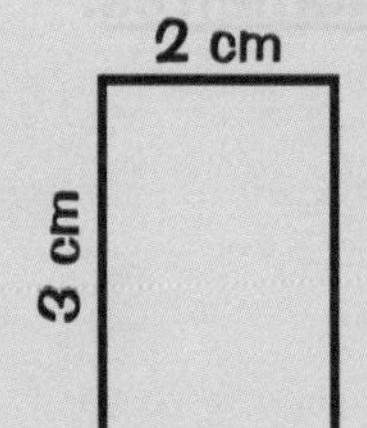

Area of the rectangle:

$3 \times 2 = \underline{6\ \text{cm}^2}$

Area of the triangle:

$\frac{1}{2} \times 3 \times 4 = \underline{6\ \text{cm}^2}$

So the total area is 6 + 6 = 12 cm².

"I can calculate the area of a triangle."

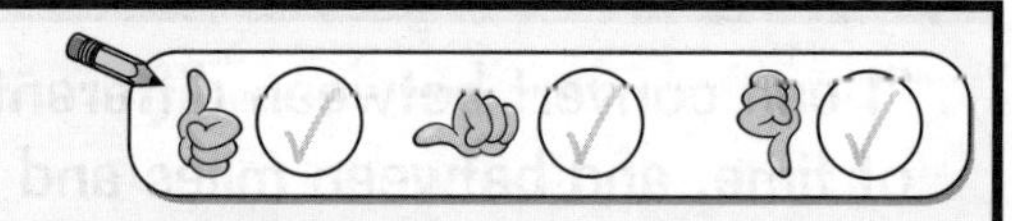

Area of a Parallelogram

Area of a Parallelogram = Base × Height

If you need to find the area of a parallelogram, use this rule:

Area of Parallelogram = Base × Height

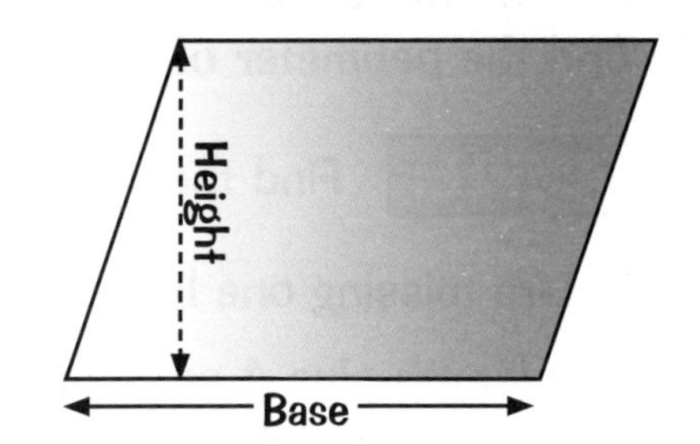

EXAMPLES:

a) Find the area of this parallelogram.

$3 \times 5 = 15\ cm^2$

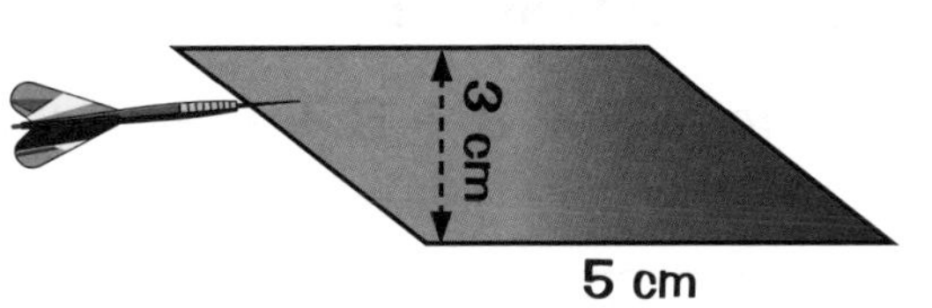

b) Jane makes a giant parallelogram shaped cookie.
Find its area.
Do $12 \times 25 = 300\ cm^2$

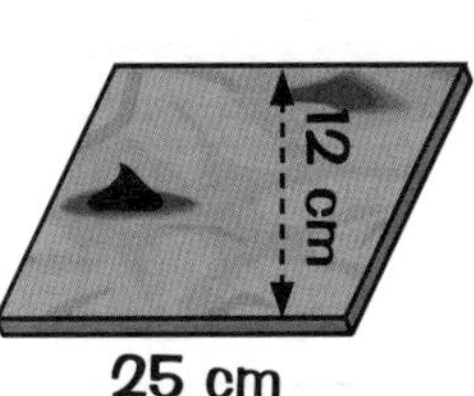

$$\begin{array}{r} 25 \\ \times\ 12 \\ \hline 50 \\ 250 \\ \hline 300 \end{array}$$

EXAMPLE: My garden is a parallelogram.
At the side there is a triangular pond.
What area of my garden is grass?

Find the area of the parallelogram first, then subtract the area of the pond.

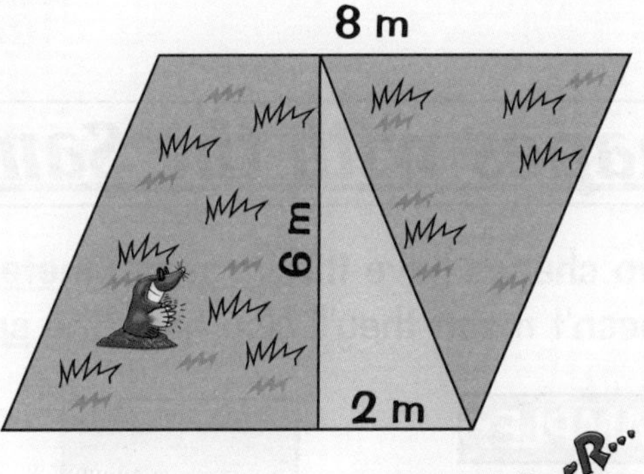

The garden is a parallelogram.
So its area $= 8 \times 6 = 48\ m^2$

The pond is a triangle.
So its area $= \frac{1}{2} \times 2 \times 6 = 6\ m^2$

Subtract the area of the pond from the area of the garden.
$48 - 6 = 42\ m^2$

The grassy part of my garden has an area of $42\ m^2$.

"I can calculate the area of a parallelogram."

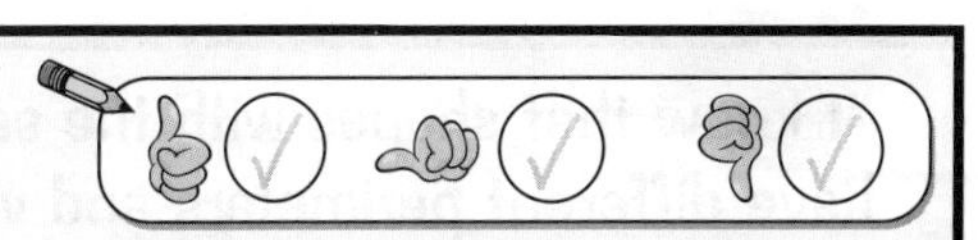

Perimeters and Areas

Finding the Perimeters of Shapes

The perimeter is the distance around the outside of a shape.
To find the perimeter of a shape, add up the lengths of all the sides.

EXAMPLE: Find the perimeter of the shape on the right.

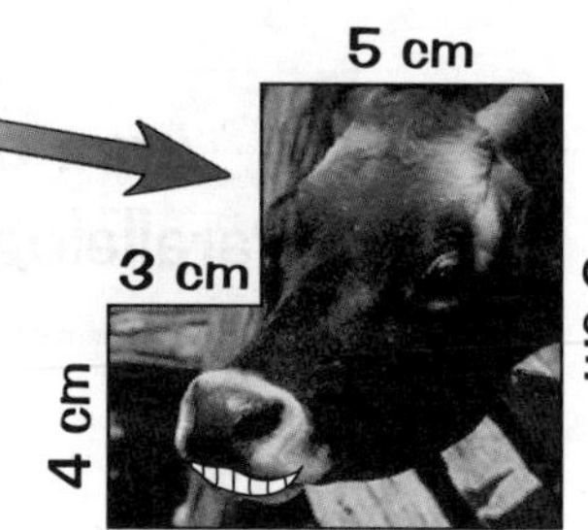

You're missing one length.

This length plus 4 cm must be the same length as the opposite side, which is 8 cm.
So the missing side must be 8 – 4 = 4 cm long.

The perimeter is 5 + 8 + 8 + 4 + 3 + 4 = 32 cm.

Shapes with the Same Area can have Different Perimeters

If two shapes have the same area it doesn't mean they'll also have the same perimeter.

EXAMPLE:

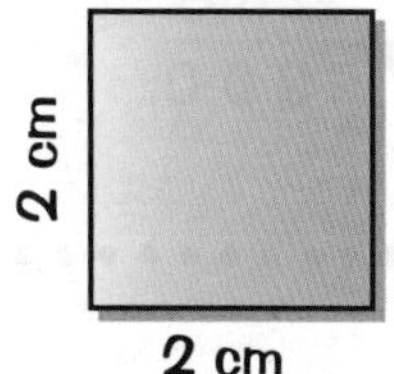

Area = 2×2 = 4 cm^2

Perimeter = 2 + 2 + 2 + 2 = 8 cm

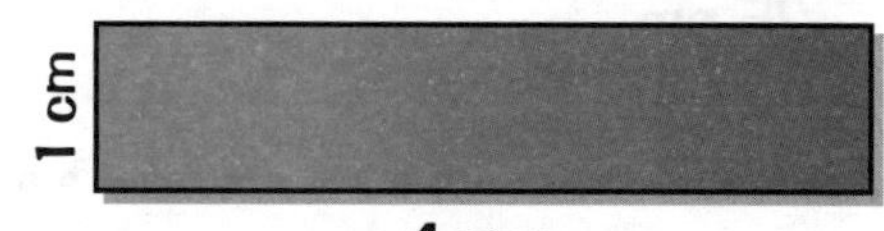

Area = 4×1 = 4 cm^2

Perimeter = 4 + 1 + 4 + 1 = 10 cm

Shapes with the Same Perimeter can have Different Areas

If two shapes have the same perimeter it doesn't mean they'll also have the same area.

EXAMPLE:

Perimeter = 3 + 3 + 3 + 3 = 12 cm

Area = 3×3 = 9 cm^2

Perimeter = 4 + 2 + 4 + 2 = 12 cm

Area = 4×2 = 8 cm^2

"I know that shapes with the same area can have different perimeters and vice versa."

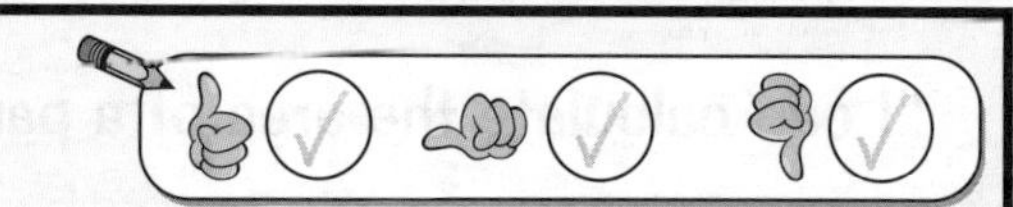

Volumes of Cubes and Cuboids

You Can Find Volume by Counting Cubes

The volume of a shape is the amount of space it takes up.

Say you've got a cuboid made up of cubes with sides of 1 cm.

The number of cubes is the same as the volume of your cuboid.

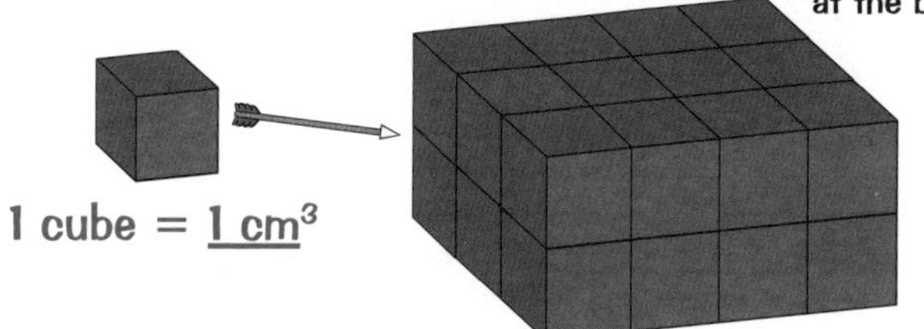

There's a Formula for Calculating Volume

There's a quicker way of working out the volume of cubes and cuboids by measuring the lengths of the sides:

It's the same formula for cubes too.

Volume of Cuboid = Length × Width × Height

$$V = L \times W \times H$$

EXAMPLE: Find the volume of this cuboid.

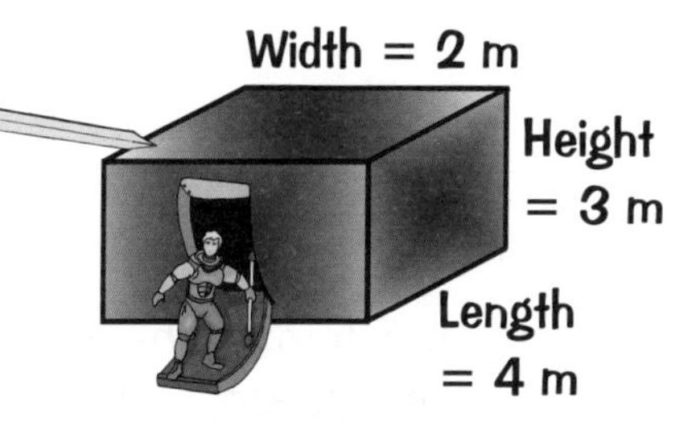

Volume = length × width × height

= 4 × 2 × 3 = 24 m³

EXAMPLE: Calculate the volume of land shown below.

The land can be split into two cuboids.
Work out the volume of each then add them together.

Volume of left-hand cuboid = 2 × 2 × 2 = 8 km³

Volume of right-hand cuboid = 1 × 3 × 2 = 6 km³

So the total volume = 8 + 6 = 14 km³

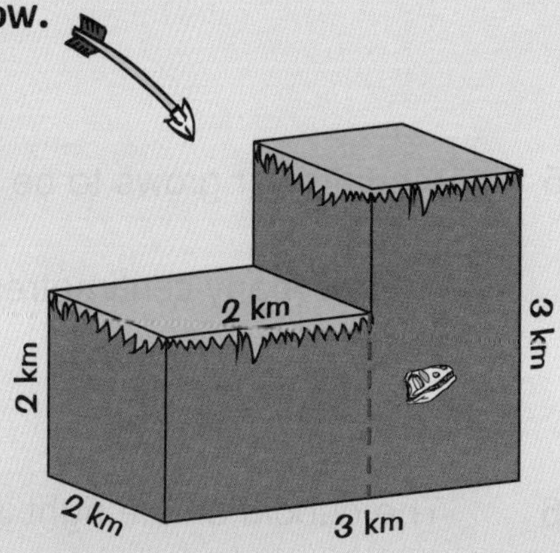

"I can calculate the volumes of cubes and cuboids."

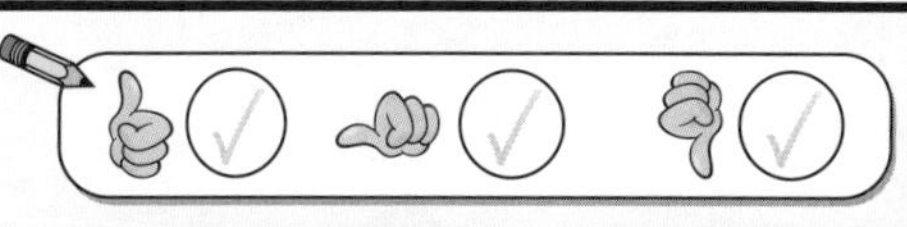

Practice Questions

Start off with the green questions — they're the easiest ones.
The blue ones are a bit harder, and the pink ones are the hardest.

1 A bottle of potato juice contains 1056 ml of juice.

How much is this in litres?

2 Find the area of these shapes.

a)

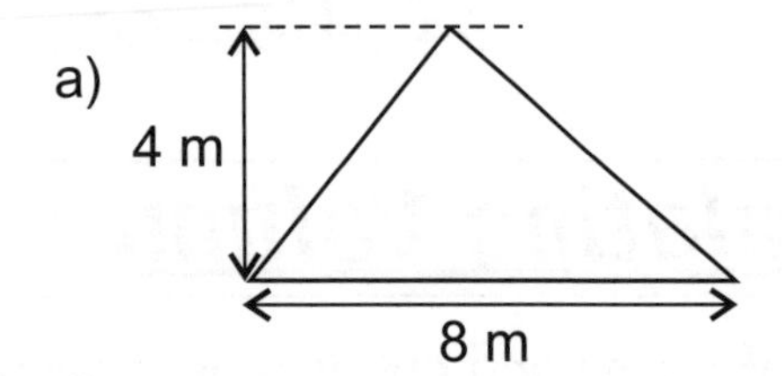

b)

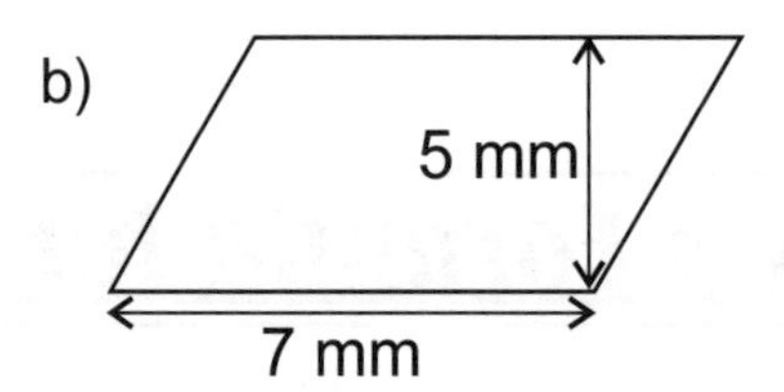

3 Find the perimeter of the shape to the right.

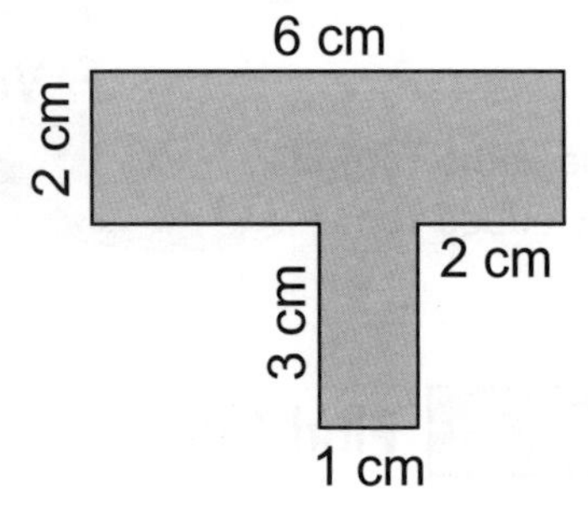

4 Andy and Tom are having a running contest.
Andy runs 32 km. Tom runs 22 miles.

Who runs the furthest?

5 A sunflower grows to be 1.65 metres tall. Maya is 143 centimetres tall.

How many centimetres taller is the sunflower than Maya?

6 The cuboid on the right is made up of 1 cm^3 cubes.

Calculate the volume of the cuboid.

Practice Questions

7 A box of chocolates contains 5 chocolates and has a mass of 0.1 kg. The empty box has a mass of 0.025 kg.

Calculate the mass of one chocolate. Give your answer in grams.

8 Alan is going on holiday for a week.

How many hours is this?

9 Calculate the volume of the cuboid on the right.

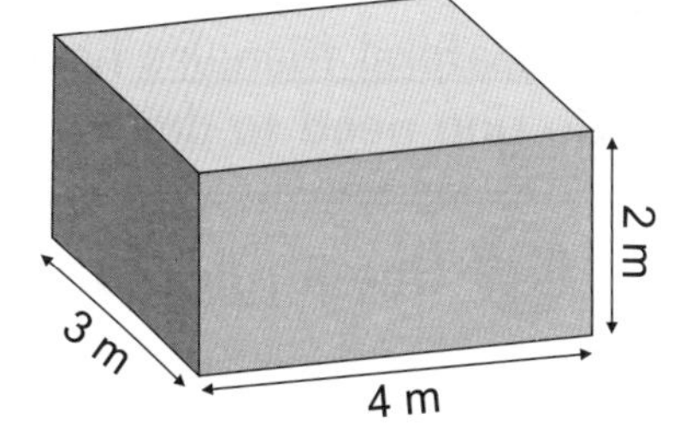

10 Kirstie is making a patchwork quilt. One of the pieces of material is shown on the right. It is a rectangle with four identical triangles removed.

Find the area of the piece of material.

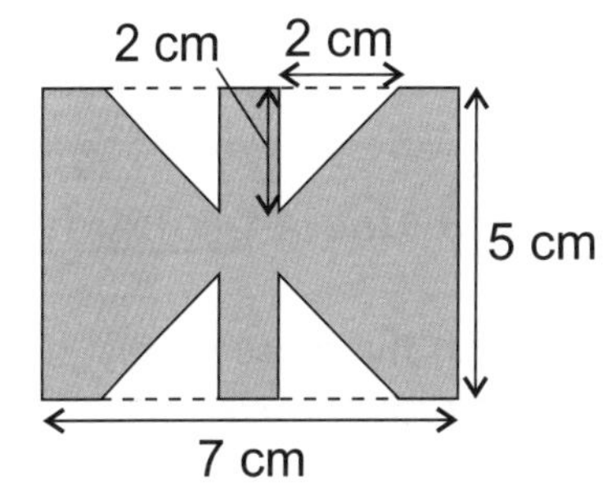

11 A plastic bead is in the shape of a cuboid with a cuboid-shaped hole through its length.

Find the volume of plastic used to make the bead.

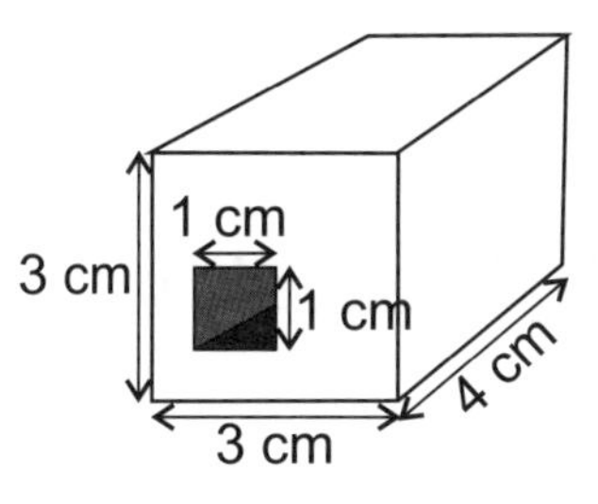

12 A rectangle has an area of 15 cm^2 and length of 5 cm.

a) What is its perimeter?

b) Draw another rectangle with an area of 15 cm^2. Label the lengths of its sides and calculate its perimeter.

Drawing 2D Shapes

Use the Right Tools to Draw 2D Shapes

To draw 2D shapes accurately you need...

A protractor — to measure angles.

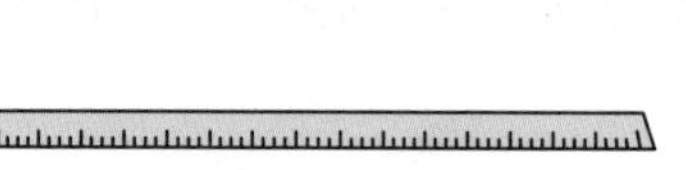

A ruler — to measure lengths.

A sharp pencil.

EXAMPLE: Draw an equilateral triangle with sides of 4 cm.

Equilateral triangles have sides the same length and angles the same size.
So you need to draw a triangle where each side is 4 cm long and each angle is 60°.

1. Use a ruler to measure and draw your first line.

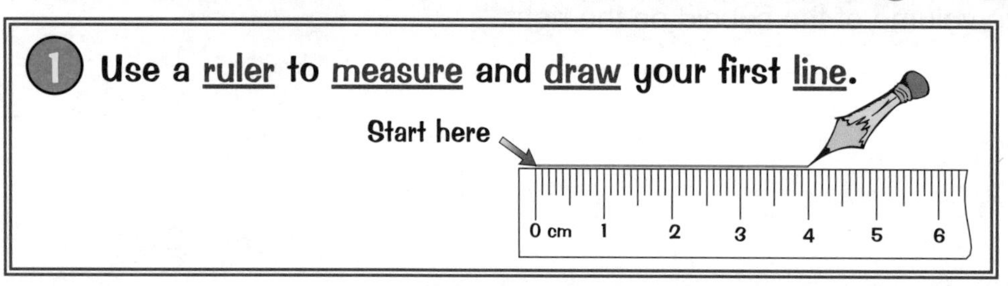

2. Use a protractor to draw your first angle.

Put the cross on the protractor over the end of your line. Line up the bottom line on the protractor with your line.

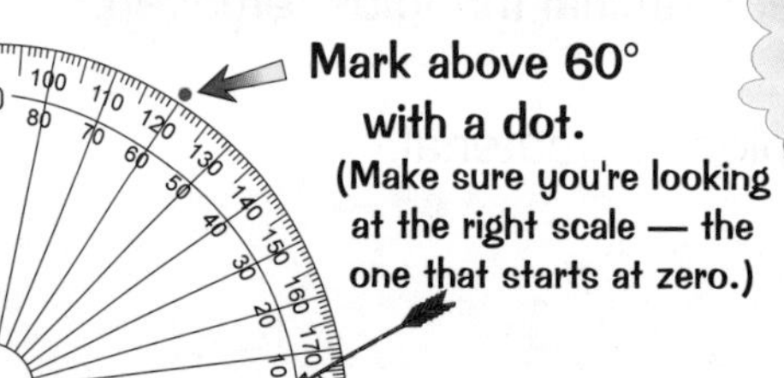

Mark above 60° with a dot.
(Make sure you're looking at the right scale — the one that starts at zero.)

If your shape has right angles, you can use a set square to draw them instead.

3. Complete your shape.

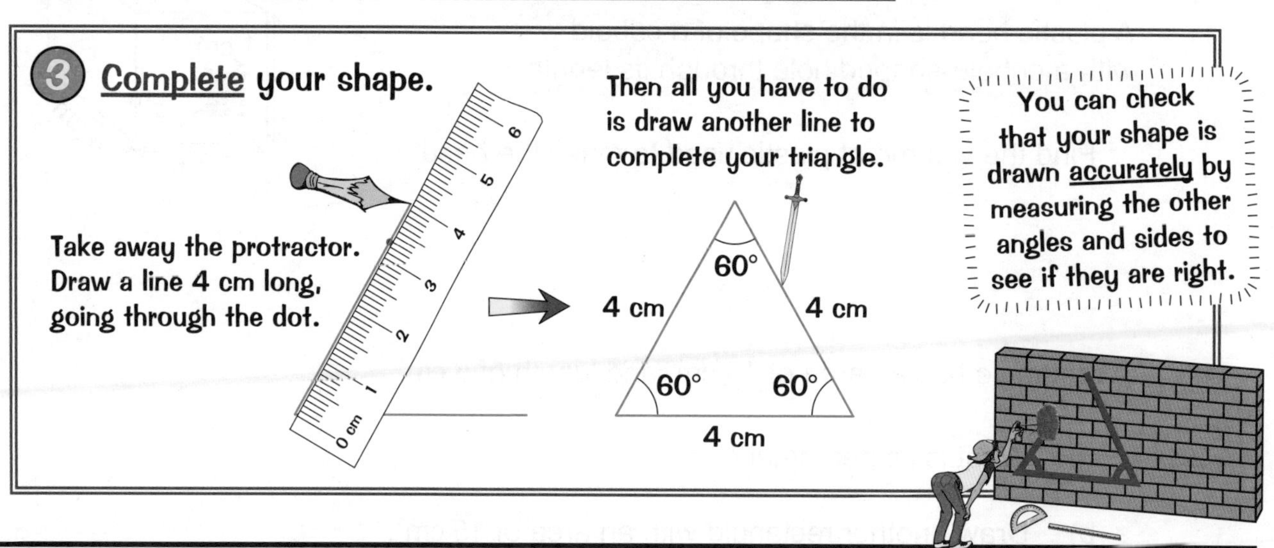

Take away the protractor. Draw a line 4 cm long, going through the dot.

Then all you have to do is draw another line to complete your triangle.

You can check that your shape is drawn accurately by measuring the other angles and sides to see if they are right.

"I can draw 2D shapes accurately."

Making 3D Shapes

You Fold a Net to make a 3D Shape

Look at the shape of each face on a 3D solid. These shapes must be part of the solid's net. There's often more than one net you can use to make a 3D shape.

EXAMPLE:

A cube has 6 square faces... So its net needs 6 squares...

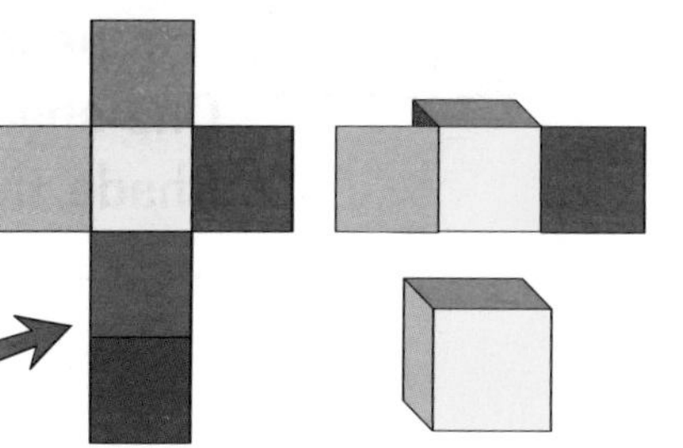

Here are some more nets of 3D shapes that you need to know:

1) Triangular Prism

4 cm
15 cm
6 cm

There are 2 triangular faces, so 2 parts of the net must be triangles.

4 cm
6 cm
5 cm
5 cm
15 cm

You can't see these three faces in the 3D picture.

Each face of the 3D shape has to match up with one part of the net.

2) Cuboid

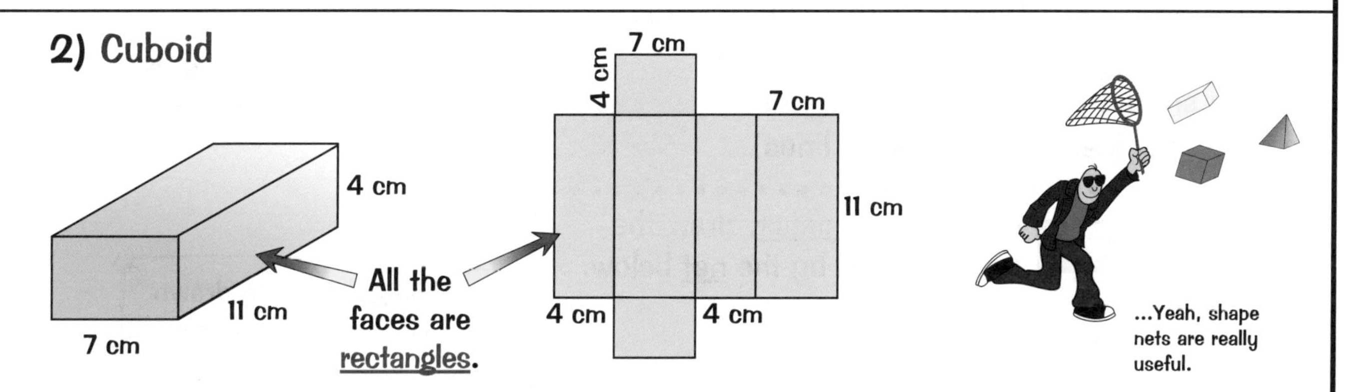

3) Pyramid

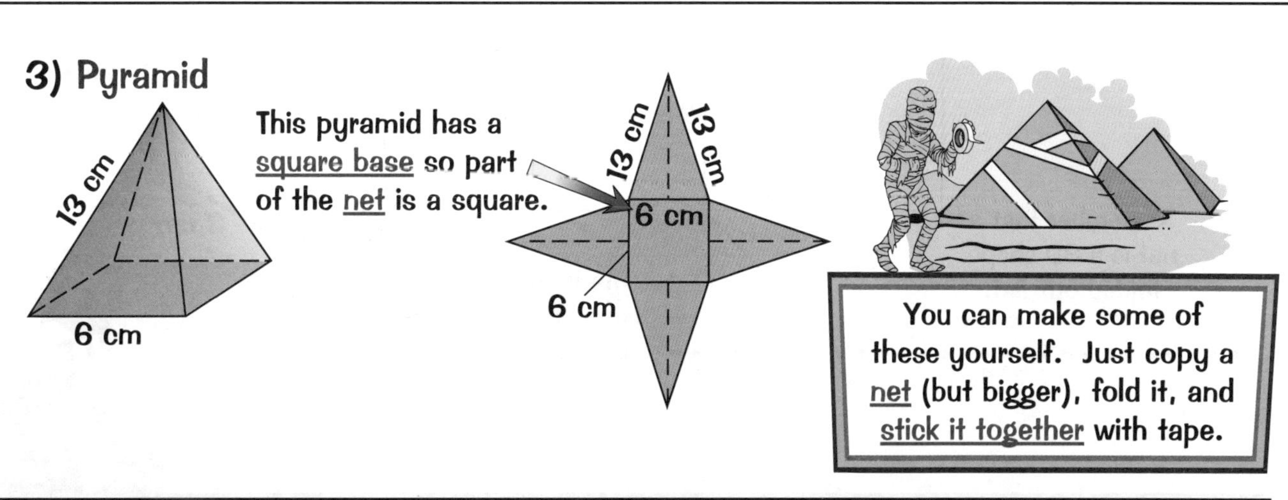

This pyramid has a square base so part of the net is a square.

You can make some of these yourself. Just copy a net (but bigger), fold it, and stick it together with tape.

"I can recognise, describe and build 3D shapes. I can make nets."

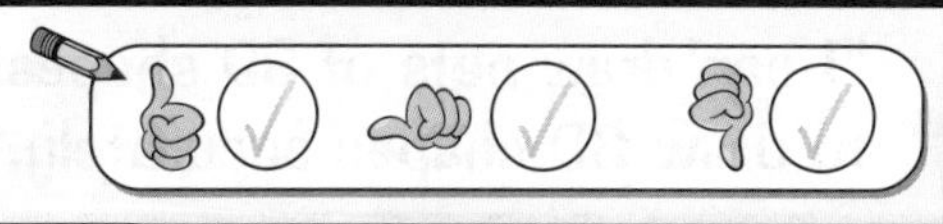

Making 3D Shapes

You Can Use Grids to Draw Nets

EXAMPLE: A cube is shaded on two of its faces, as shown. One shaded face is marked on the cube's net below. Shade the net to show the other shaded face.

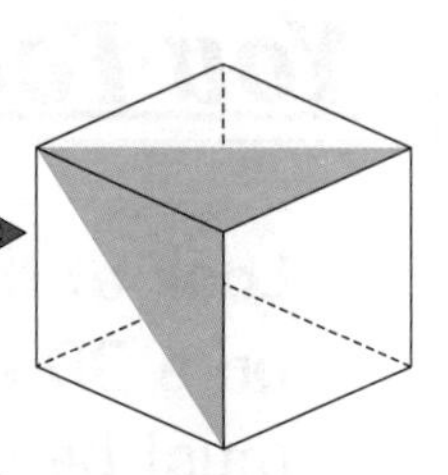

Imagine folding the net up. Work out which faces on the net meet the edge of the shaded triangle.

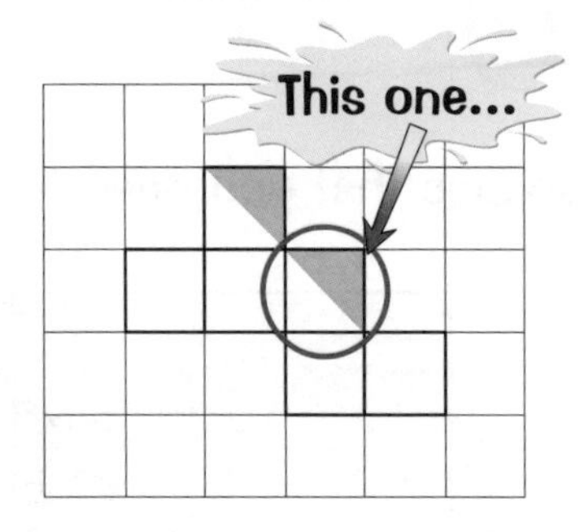

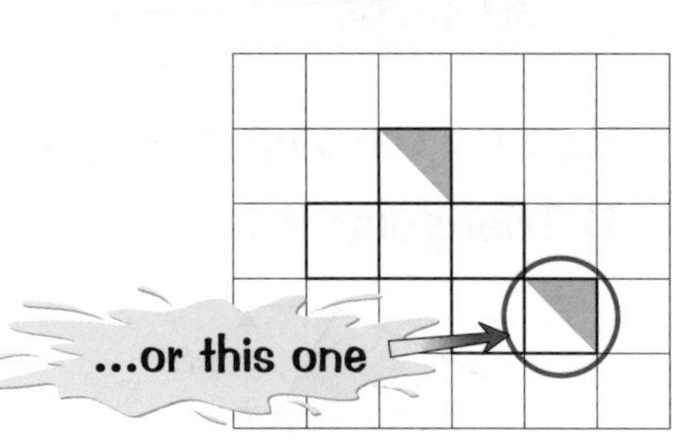

Use Isometric Paper to Draw 3D Shapes

Isometric (dotty) paper looks like this: Join the dots to draw your shape — you should ONLY draw vertical or diagonal lines (no horizontal lines).

The vertical or diagonal distance between each pair of dots represents 1 cm.

EXAMPLE: On isometric paper, draw the prism formed by the net below.

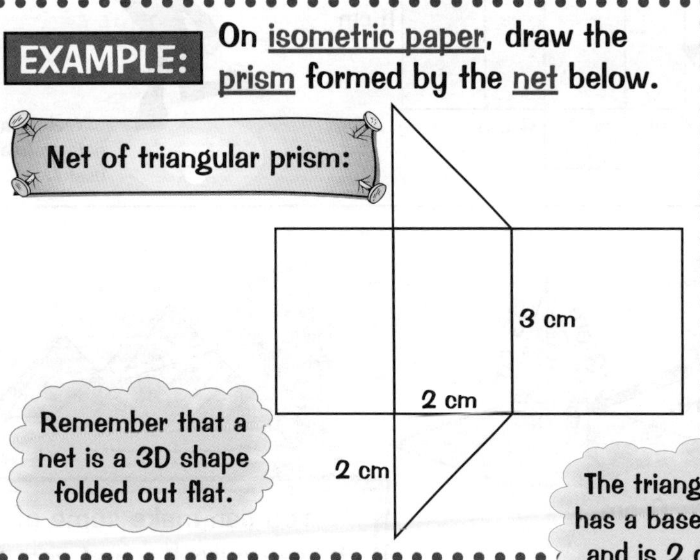

Triangular prism drawn on isometric paper:

2 cm

2 cm

3 cm

The prism is 3 cm long.

The triangular end has a base of 2 cm and is 2 cm high.

"I can draw nets of 3D shapes. I can use nets to draw 3D shapes accurately."

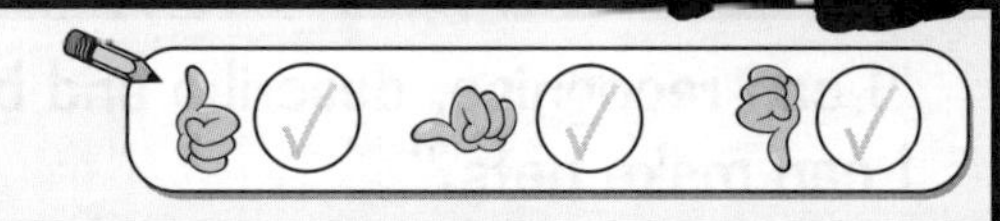

Shape Properties

Learn the Properties of These Shapes

You need to know the properties of all the shapes on this page.
Make sure that you know how to draw them all too.
Let's start with the quadrilaterals — shapes with 4 sides...

This little square means it's a right angle.

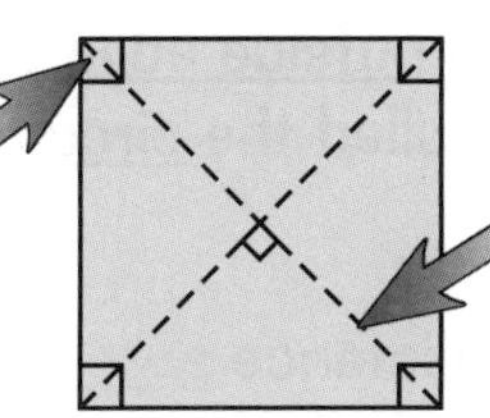

Diagonals go from one corner to the opposite corner.

RECTANGLE
2 pairs of equal-length sides
4 equal angles of 90°
2 pairs of parallel sides
2 lines of symmetry

Parallel sides are always the same distance apart and never meet.

SQUARE
4 equal-length sides
4 equal angles of 90° (right angles)
2 pairs of parallel sides
Diagonals meet at right angles
4 lines of symmetry

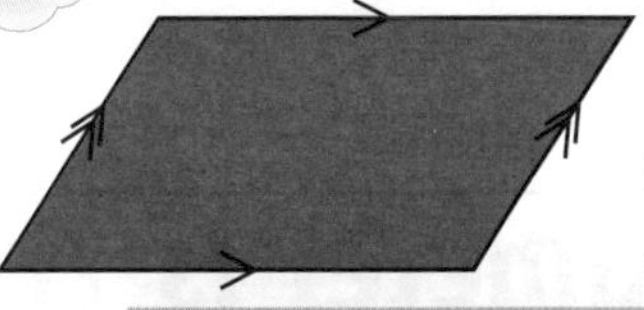

Opposite sides and opposite angles are equal.

PARALLELOGRAM
2 pairs of equal-length sides
2 pairs of equal angles
2 pairs of parallel sides
No lines of symmetry

RHOMBUS
4 equal-length sides
2 pairs of equal angles
(opposite angles are equal)
2 pairs of parallel sides
Diagonals meet at right angles
2 lines of symmetry

Matching arrows show parallel sides.

TRAPEZIUM
1 pair of parallel sides
No lines of symmetry

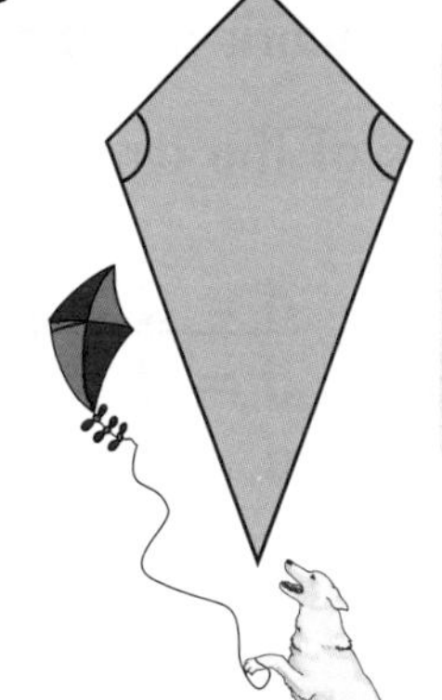

KITE
2 pairs of equal-length sides
1 pair of equal angles
No parallel sides
1 line of symmetry

You need to know the properties of the different types of triangles...

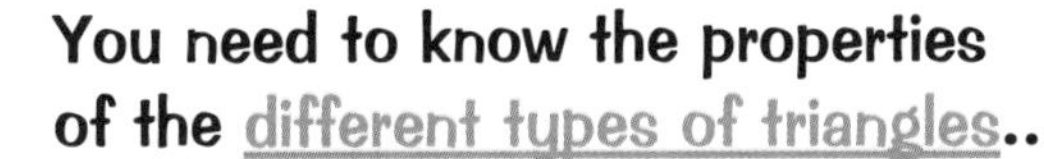

EXAMPLE:

EQUILATERAL TRIANGLE

3 equal-length sides
3 equal angles of 60°
No parallel sides
3 lines of symmetry

...and other polygons too.

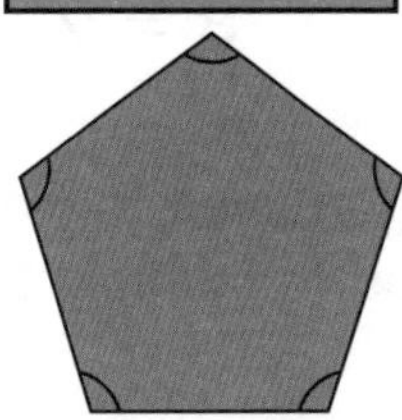

EXAMPLE: **REGULAR PENTAGON**

5 equal-length sides
5 equal angles
No parallel sides
5 lines of symmetry

"I know the properties of different shapes."

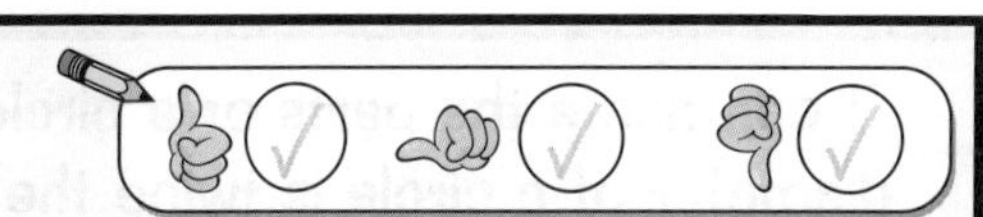

Circles

Learn the Parts of a Circle

You need to know the different parts of a circle.

The distance from the edge to the centre of the circle is called the radius.

circumference

radius

diameter

The outside edge of a circle is called the circumference.

The distance across the circle through the centre is called the diameter.

The Diameter is Twice the Radius

You can write this as $d = 2 \times r$ where d = diameter and r = radius.

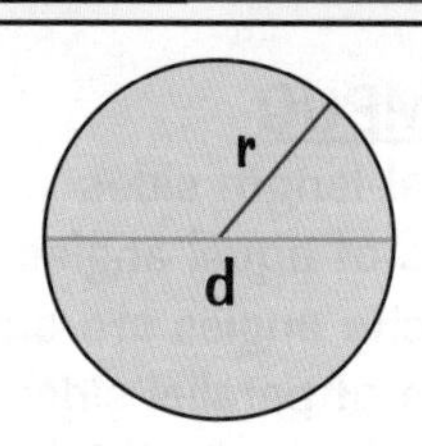

You can use $d = 2 \times r$ to work out the diameter...

EXAMPLE: The radius of the circle is 5 cm. What is the diameter of the circle?

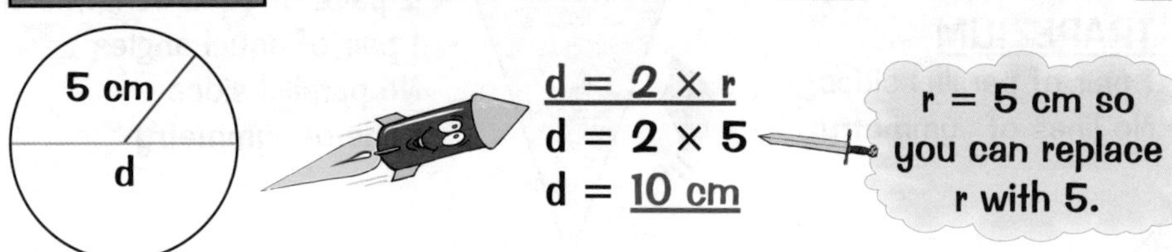

$d = 2 \times r$
$d = 2 \times 5$
$d = 10$ cm

You can also use $d = 2 \times r$ to work out the radius...

EXAMPLE: The diameter of this circle is 8 cm. What is the radius of this circle?

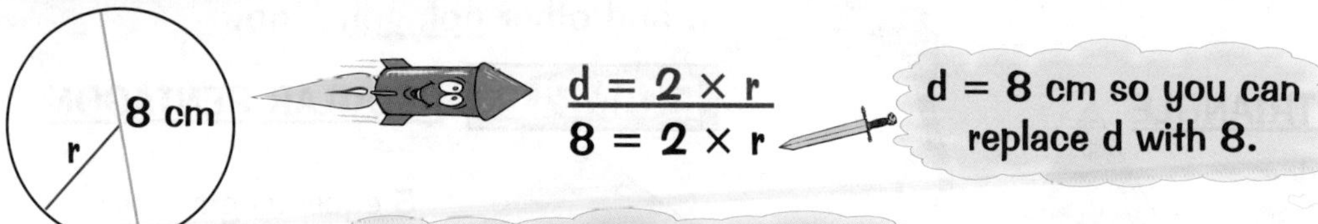

$d = 2 \times r$
$8 = 2 \times r$

Then you need to work out what you need to multiply 2 by to get 8.

$8 = 2 \times 4$
So $r = 4$ cm

"I can name the parts of a circle and I know that the diameter of a circle is twice the length of its radius."

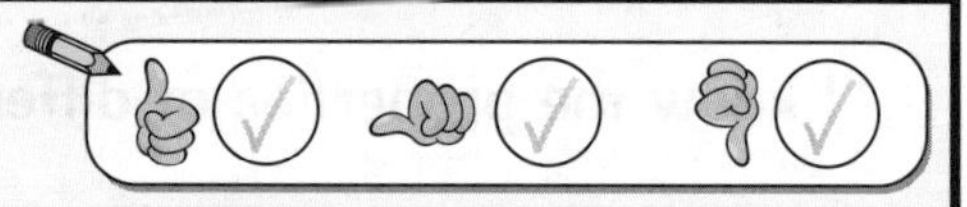

Angles in Shapes

The Angles in a Quadrilateral Add up to 360°

Quadrilaterals are 4-sided shapes. The angles in a quadrilateral add up to 360°.

EXAMPLE: Find the missing angle in the quadrilateral on the right.

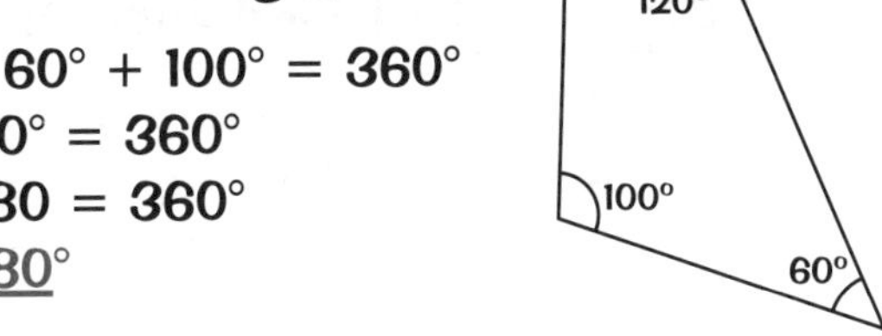

The angles will add up to 360°. → $x + 120° + 60° + 100° = 360°$

Add together the 3 angles you know: → $x + 280° = 360°$

Then you need to work out what to add to this to make 360°: → $80 + 280 = 360°$

So $x = 80°$

The Angles in a Triangle Add up to 180°

All the angles in a triangle add up to 180°.

You can use this amazing fact to work out the missing angles in triangles.

EXAMPLE: This is an equilateral cheese triangle. What is angle z?

It's an equilateral triangle so all 3 angles are equal.

So each angle will be $180 \div 3 = 60°$

EXAMPLE: This is an isosceles shark tooth. What are angles e and f?

The angles in a triangle add up to 180°. So...

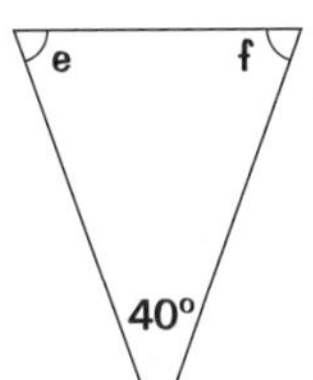

$e + f + 40 = 180$ which means that $e + f = 140$

It's an isosceles triangle so angles e and f are equal.

$140 \div 2 = 70$, so $e = 70°$ and $f = 70°$

Polygons have Interior and Exterior Angles

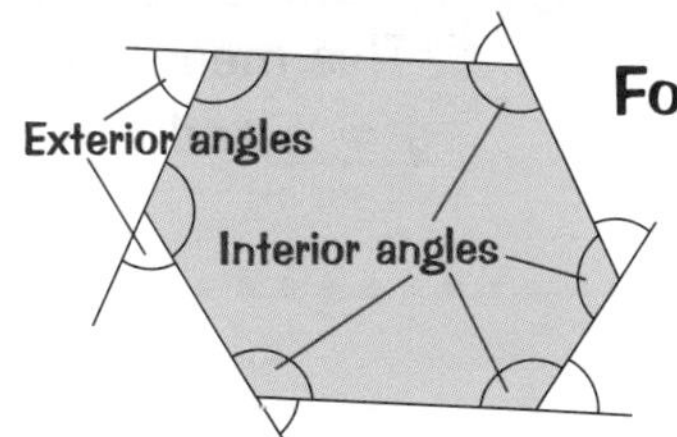

For any polygon:

- SUM OF EXTERIOR ANGLES = 360°
- INTERIOR ANGLE = 180° – EXTERIOR ANGLE
- SUM OF INTERIOR ANGLES = $(n - 2) \times 180°$

where n is the number of sides (so for a hexagon, $n = 6$)

For regular polygons ONLY:

- All exterior angles are the same.
- All interior angles are the same.
- Exterior angle = $\dfrac{360°}{n}$.

EXAMPLE: What are the interior and exterior angles of a regular pentagon?

A pentagon has 5 sides, so $n = 5$.

Exterior angle = $\dfrac{360°}{n} = \dfrac{360°}{5} = 72°$

Interior angle = $180° - 72° = 108°$

"I can use my knowledge of shapes to find missing angles."

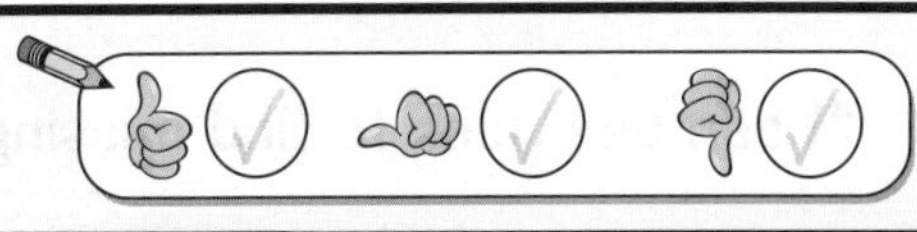

Angle Rules

The Angles Around a Point Add up to 360°

You know that the angles around a point add up to 360°.

EXAMPLE: Find angle t.

$90° + 130° + 36° + 45° + t = 360°$
$301 + t = 360°$ so $t = 59°$

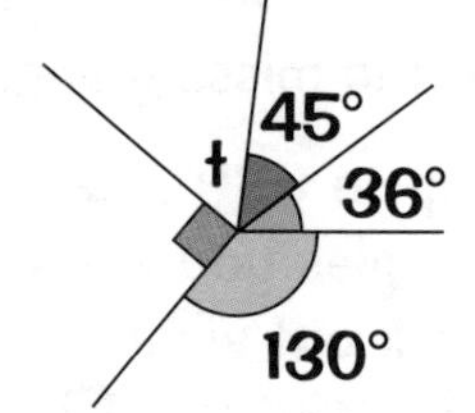

The Angles on a Straight Line Add up to 180°

You know that the angles that meet on a straight line add up to 180°.

EXAMPLE: Find angle s.

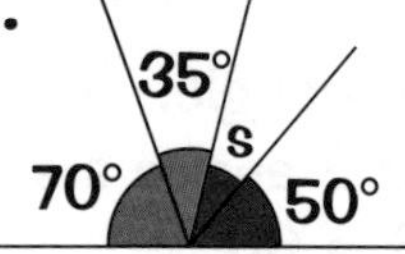

$70° + 35° + 50° + s = 180°$
$155 + s = 180$ so $s = 25°$

Vertically Opposite Angles are Equal

When two lines cross you get two pairs of opposite angles.
These are called vertically opposite angles.
Vertically opposite angles are equal.

a and c are vertically opposite angles.

b and d are vertically opposite angles.

a b d c

This means that $a = c$ and $b = d$.

EXAMPLE: $f = 40°$. What is g?

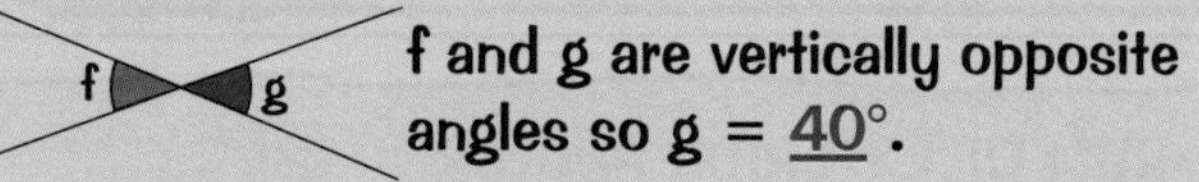

f and g are vertically opposite angles so $g = 40°$.

EXAMPLE: $z = 50°$. Find angles w, x and y.

x w z y

z and w are equal as they are vertically opposite angles, so $w = 50°$.
Angles on a straight line add up to 180°.
z and x are on a straight line.
So... $z + x = 180°$
$50 + x = 180°$
$x = 130°$

$x + y$ are vertically opposite angles, so they are equal.
This means $y = 130°$.

w, x, y and z are around a point so your angles should add up to 360°.

"I can use rules to find missing angles."

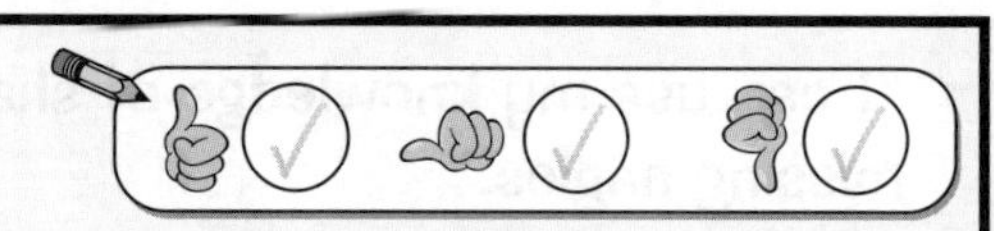

Coordinates

A Point is Identified by its Coordinates

A point has two numbers to identify its position: its coordinates. They're always put in brackets like this: (8, 9).

Coordinates tell you how many across and how many up or down from the origin (0, 0) a point is.

Make sure you put the x and y coordinates in the right order. You always go across first, so the x coordinate comes first.

Grids are Split into Four Quadrants

Each quarter of this diagram is called a quadrant — there are 4 quadrants altogether.

The numbers on the axes tell you where the point is compared to the origin — they give you the coordinates of the point:

(x, y)

- x: If this number is positive it means the point is to the right of the origin. If this number is negative it means the point is to the left of the origin.
- y: If this number is positive it means the point is above the origin. If this number is negative it means the point is below the origin.

EXAMPLES:

From your point, draw a vertical line to the x-axis to find the x-coordinate and a horizontal line to the y-axis to find the y-coordinate.

The coordinates of the points above are: A (2, 3) B (–2, 3) C (–2, –3) D (2, –3)

You Can Work Out Missing Coordinates

You can use what you know about shapes to work out missing coordinates.

EXAMPLE:

This shape is a parallelogram. Find the coordinates of Point D.

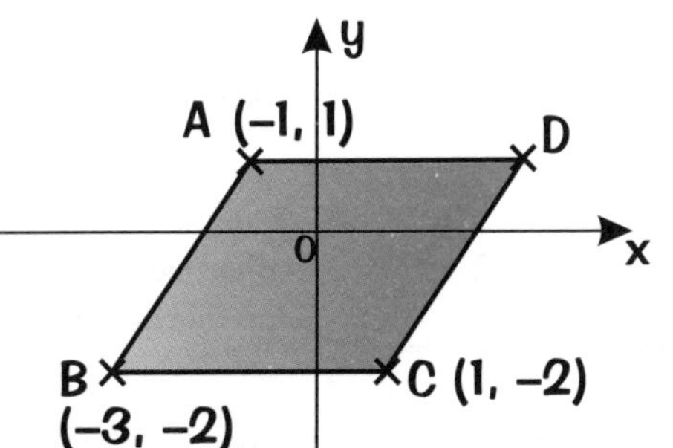

Point D is in line horizontally with Point A — so it must have the same y-coordinate. It's 1.

Parallelograms have equal-length sides so you know that side AD is the same length as side BC.

The x-coordinate of B is –3 and the x-coordinate of C is 1. So C is 4 units to the right of B.
D must be 4 units to the right of A.
The x-coordinate of A is –1, and –1 + 4 = 3.
So the x-coordinate of D is 3.

So D's coordinates must be (3, 1).

"I can use coordinates in four quadrants."

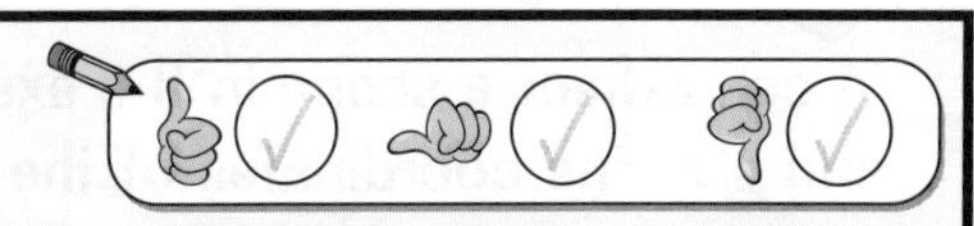

Reflection

Reflection in a Line

You can reflect shapes and patterns in a mirror line.

Each point and its reflection are exactly the same distance from the mirror line.

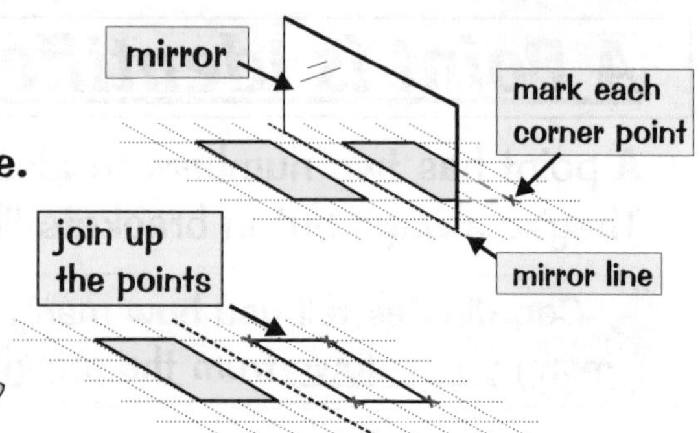

You Can Use an Axis as a Mirror Line

You can reflect a shape in the axis of a grid. You need to count how many units each point is from the axis (the mirror line). Then, on the other side of the axis, count the same number of units away and draw the reflected point.

EXAMPLE: Reflect shape A in the y-axis. Label the reflected shape B.
Find the coordinates of the image of vertex Z.

The image is just the transformed shape.

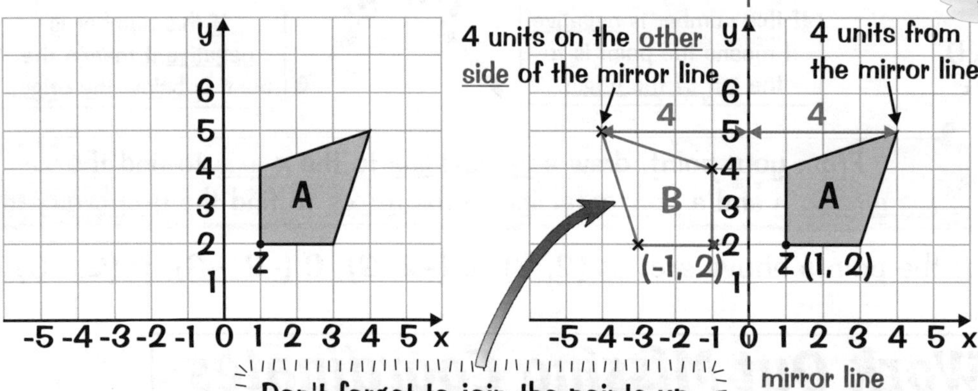

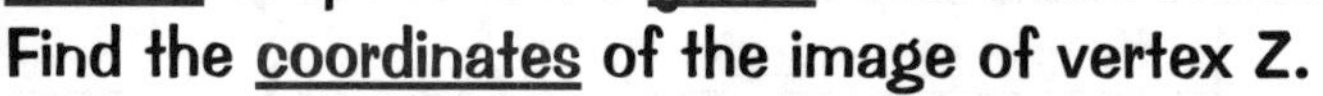

The coordinates of the image of vertex Z: (-1, 2)

EXAMPLE:

Reflect shape F using the x-axis as a mirror line.
Label the reflected shape G.
Find the coordinates of the image of vertex Q.

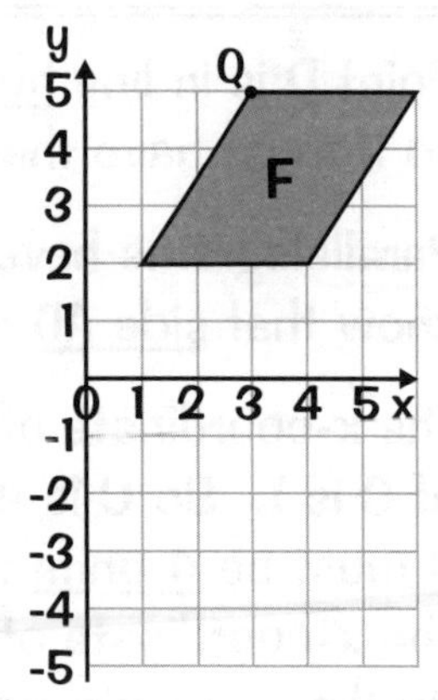

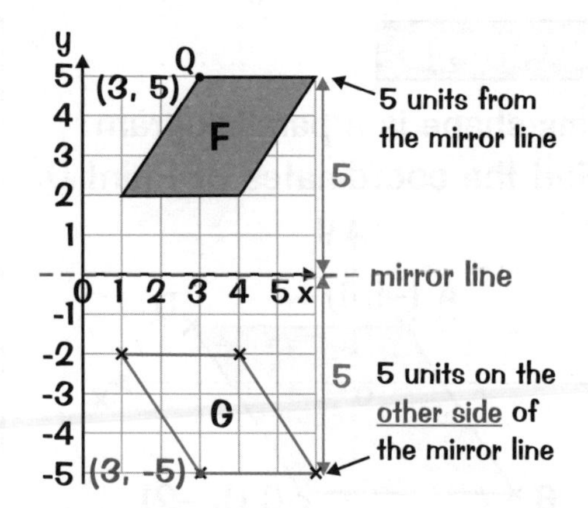

The coordinates of the image of vertex Q: (3, -5)

"I can reflect a shape in the axes of a grid and give the coordinates of the image."

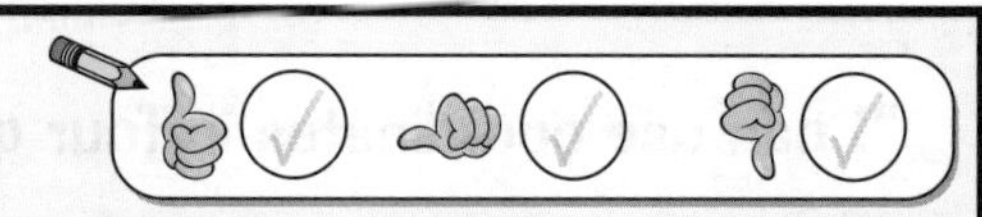

Translation

Translation is Sliding

Translation is when a shape slides from one place to another, without rotating or flipping over.

EXAMPLE: Translate this shape 3 squares down and 1 square to the left.

For each vertex, go 3 squares down, 1 square to the left and mark a cross. Then just join up the crosses.

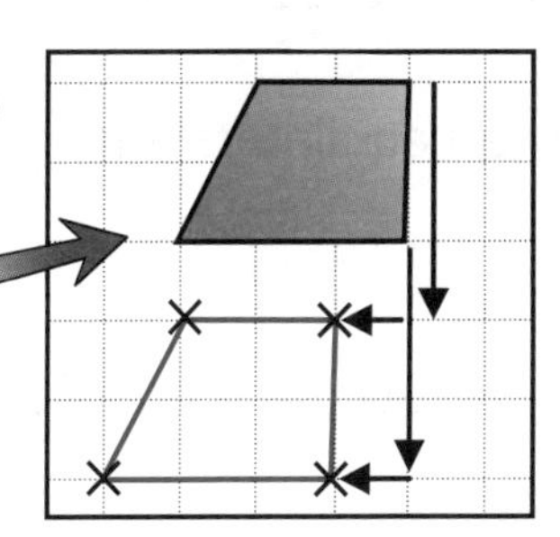

Translating Shapes on Grids

A shape can slide left, right, up or down. A negative number means you move the shape left or down (so a horizontal translation of -2 goes left).

EXAMPLE:

Translate shape C -4 units horizontally and +3 units vertically. Label the translated shape D. Find the coordinates of the translated vertex W on shape D.

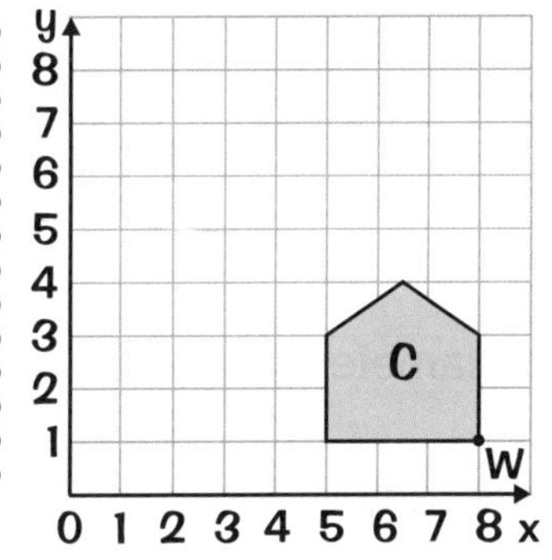

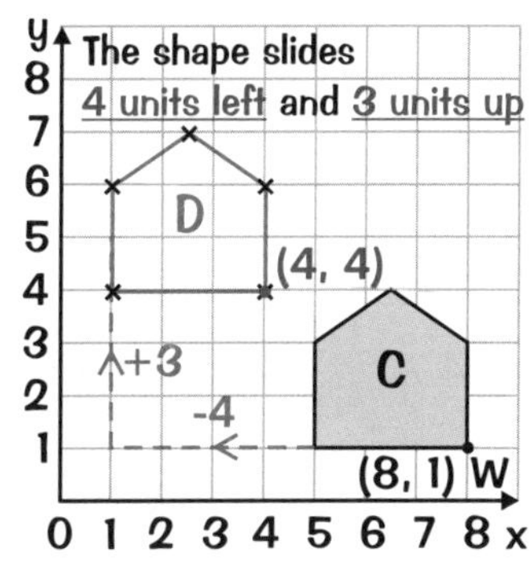

EXAMPLE:

The coordinates of vertex P on shape R = (a, b). Shape R is translated so that the coordinates of the translated vertex P are (a – 2, b – 3). Find the coordinates of the translated vertex P.

There are two ways you can do this...

1. You could do the translation to find the coordinates. Translating vertex P from (a, b) to (a – 2, b – 3) means translating 2 units left and 3 units down. So the coordinates of the translated vertex P are (3, 1).

2. You could do it using the coordinates. The coordinates of vertex P are (5, 4). So (a, b) = (5, 4). The coordinates of the translated vertex P are (a – 2, b – 3), which is (5 – 2, 4 – 3). So the coordinates of the translated vertex P are (3, 1).

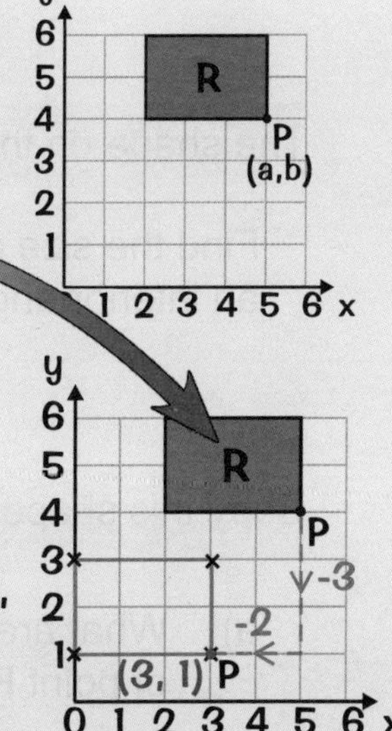

"I can translate shapes using coordinates."

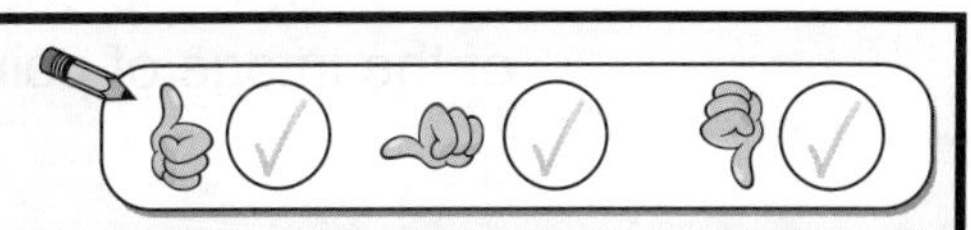

Practice Questions

Start off with the green questions — they're the easiest ones.
The blue ones are a bit harder, and the pink ones are the hardest.

1 Draw an equilateral triangle with sides of 5 cm.

2 Draw an accurate net of the cube to the right.

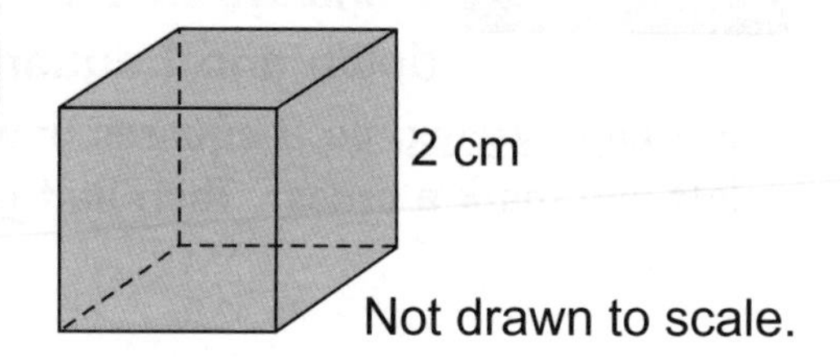

3 What is the size of angle y in this triangle?

y
48°
Not drawn to scale.

4 This circle has a diameter of 20 cm.

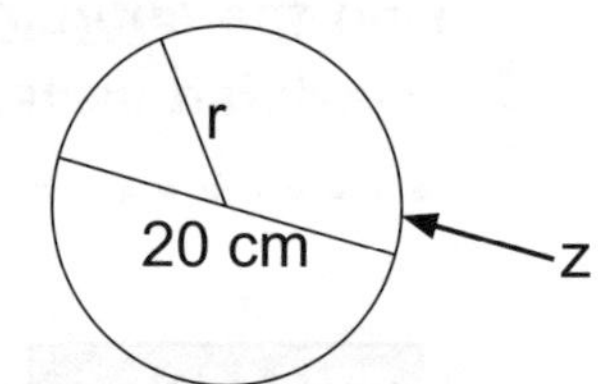

Not drawn to scale.

a) What is the radius of the circle?

b) What is the name of the part of the circle labelled z?

5 The shape on the right is a regular hexagon.

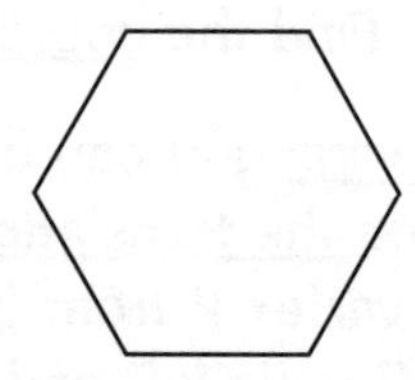

Find the size of an exterior and an interior angle in this shape.

6 Copy this shape onto a grid with labelled axes.

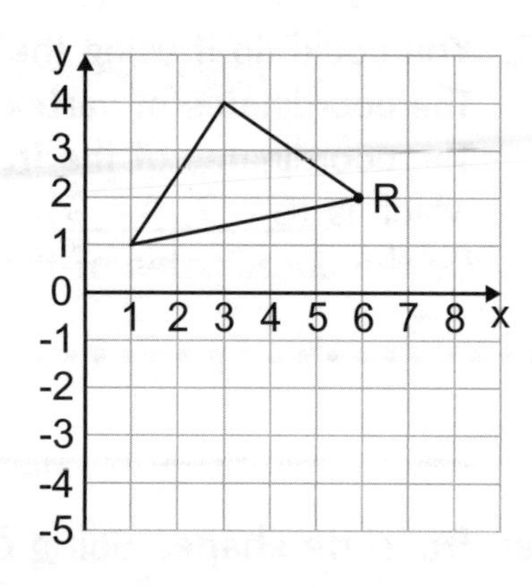

a) What are the coordinates of point R?

b) Reflect the shape in the x-axis.

c) Write down the coordinates of the image of point R.

Practice Questions

7 Copy this shape onto a grid with labelled axes.

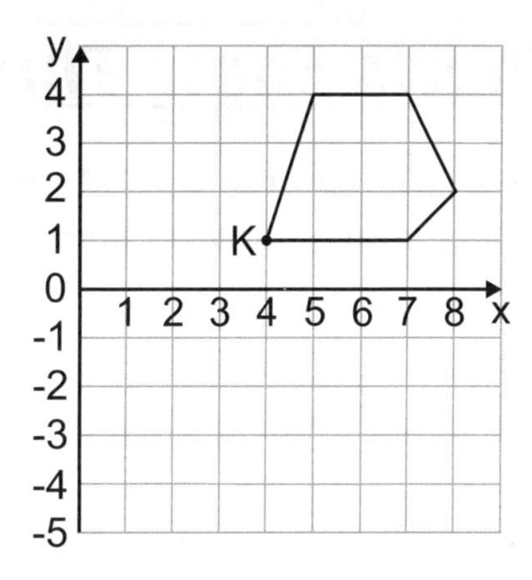

a) Translate the shape -2 units horizontally and -4 units vertically.

b) Write down the coordinates of the translated vertex K.

8 The net of a cuboid is shown on the right.

On isometric paper, draw the shape this net makes.

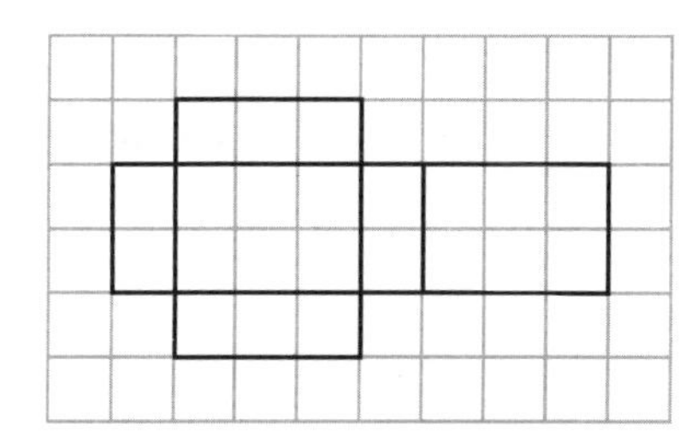

9 Look at the parallelogram on the right. Work out the size of angle x

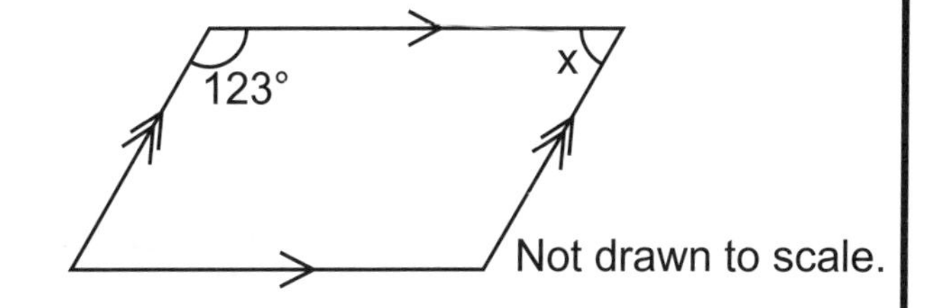

10 n = 20°. Find angles m, o and p.

Not drawn to scale.

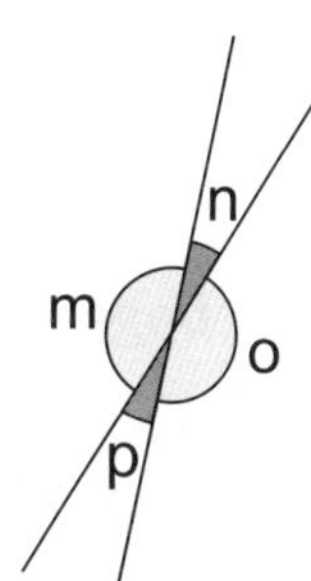

11 Jack draws the kite on the right.

Work out the coordinates of point C.

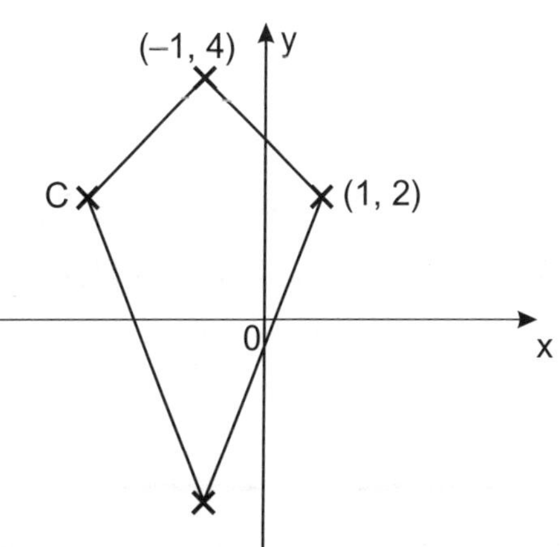

Pie Charts

Pie Charts Show Things as Proportions

Bertie Entwhistle spends 6 hours at work every day.
This pie chart shows how he spends his time.

Each coloured slice is called a "sector".
The size of each sector tells you how much of his time he spends doing different things.

Nostril Spotting
Sleeping
Eating
Mango Hammering

You can see that Bertie spends a quarter of the time sleeping. A quarter of 6 hours is 1.5 hours.

He spends half his time mango hammering. Half of 6 hours is 3 hours.

The Angles in a Pie Chart Add Up to 360°

The most important thing you should remember about pie charts is that there are 360° in a whole circle.
And that gives you this very important rule.

TOTAL of everything = 360°

EXAMPLE: A group of students was asked what their favourite animal was. The results are shown in the pie chart.

Dogs 160°
Mice 120°
Cats

The biggest sector (160°) is 'dogs'. So more students chose dogs than mice or cats.

The next biggest sector (120°) is 'mice', so this was the second most popular animal.

'Cats' is the smallest sector so is the least popular. You can work out how big the sector is by subtracting the angles of the other sectors from 360°.

360° – 160° – 120° = 80° So the angle of the cats sector is 80°.

"I understand what pie charts show."

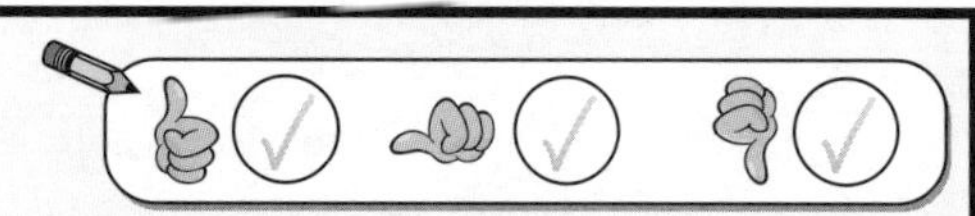

Pie Charts

Work Out Angles Using a Multiplier

To draw a pie chart, you need to turn numbers of things into angles.

EXAMPLE: This table shows the numbers of different animals in a petting zoo. Draw a pie chart to show the information.

Animal	Geese	Hamsters	Guinea pigs	Rabbits	Ducks
Number	12	20	17	15	26

1. Find the total number of things in the table.

   $12 + 20 + 17 + 15 + 26 = 90$ animals

2. 'Everything = 360°' so find the multiplier that turns your total number into 360°.

   Multiplier = $360 \div 90 = 4$
   (so each animal is represented by 4°)

3. So, to find the angle for each sector, multiply every number by 4.

Animal	Geese	Hamsters	Guinea pigs	Rabbits	Ducks	Total
Number	12	20	17	15	26	90
Angle	$12 \times 4 = 48°$	$20 \times 4 = 80°$	$17 \times 4 = 68°$	$15 \times 4 = 60°$	$26 \times 4 = 104°$	360°

4. Draw your pie chart accurately using a protractor and label each sector.

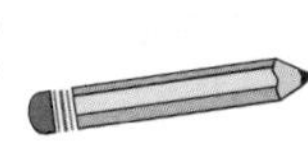

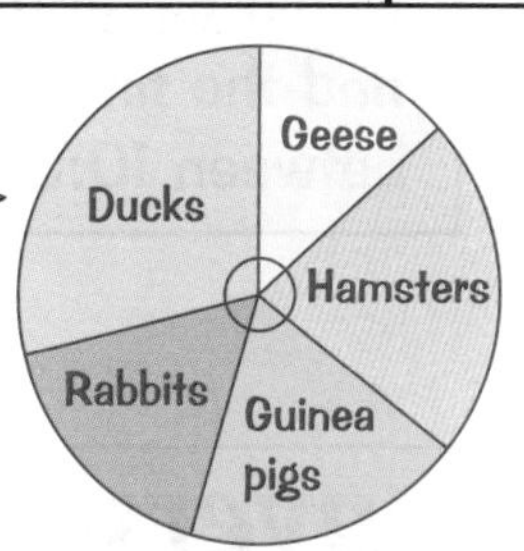

Interpreting Pie Charts

To interpret a pie chart, you need to do the opposite — turn angles into numbers. You do this by working out the angle as a fraction or a percentage of the chart.

EXAMPLE: Take the 'Geese' sector from the petting zoo example...

Measure the angle of the sector. → Geese sector = 48°

Turn it into a fraction of the chart. (Or the percentage of the chart.) → Whole chart = 360°, so the fraction is: $\frac{48}{360} = \frac{2}{15}$ (÷ 24)

Find this fraction of the total number. (Or the percentage of the total number.) → $\frac{2}{15} \times 90$ animals = 12 geese

"I can draw and interpret pie charts."

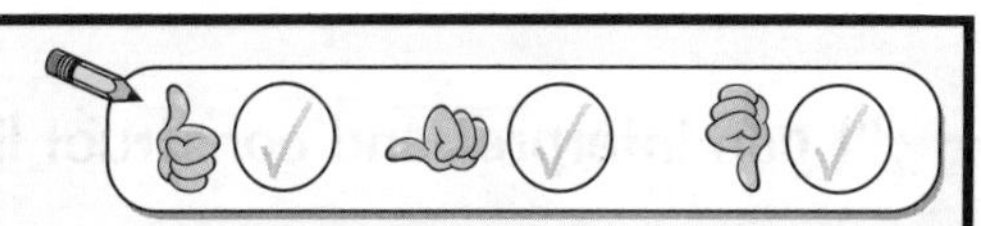

Line Graphs

Drawing Line Graphs

A line graph is a good way to show how something changes.

EXAMPLE: Nia measures the volume of rainwater in a bucket in her garden. Her results are in the table. Draw a line graph to show the data.

Time	9:00	9:30	10:00	10:30	11:00	11:30	12:00
Volume	90 ml	100 ml	120 ml	150 ml	240 ml	240 ml	240 ml

To plot the points, read up from the time and then across from the volume. Mark a cross where the two lines meet.

When you've plotted all the points, join them up with a line.

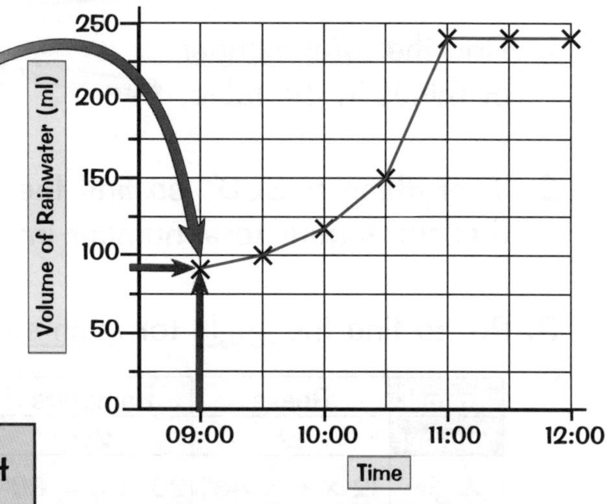

You can use the graph to answer questions about the rainfall.

Q: When was the rain heaviest?

A: When the rain was heaviest, the bucket would fill up more quickly, so you need to find the time that the volume of the bucket increased the most. This is between 10:30 and 11:00. You can tell this because the line is steepest here.

Conversion Graphs Swap Between Units

Conversion graphs help you convert between different units. One unit goes along the horizontal axis and the other goes up the vertical axis.

EXAMPLE: This conversion graph converts between miles and kilometres. How many miles is 8 km?

1. Find 8 km on the km axis, then draw a straight line across to the red line.
2. Change direction and draw a straight line down to the other axis.
3. Read off the number of miles. So 8 km = 5 miles.

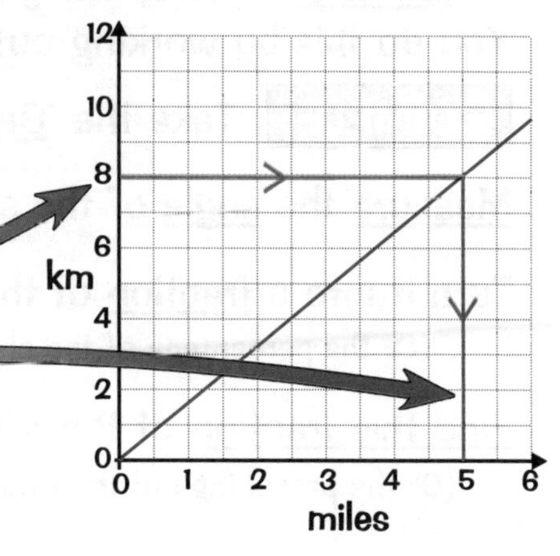

"I can interpret and construct line graphs."

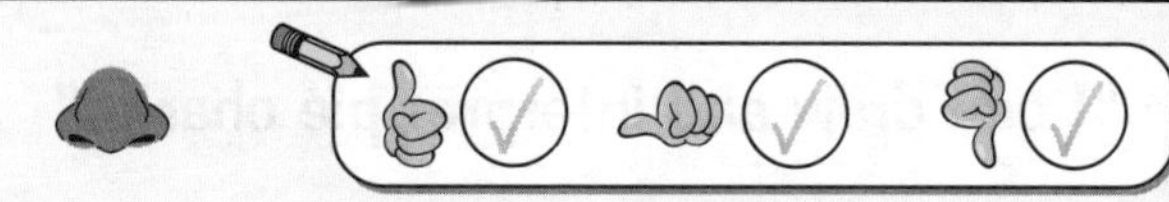

The Mean

The Mean — Add then Divide

The mean is often just called the "average". If someone asks "What's the average of these tiddlywink scores?", they probably want to know the mean.

To Work Out the Mean

1. Add up all the numbers.
2. Divide the total by how many numbers there are.

EXAMPLE: I bought 4 presents last Christmas. The table shows how much they cost. What was the mean cost of a present?

First add up the numbers:

1p + 13p + 8p + 2p = 24p

There are 4 numbers, so now just divide the total by 4:

24p ÷ 4 = 6p.

So the mean cost was 6p.

Present	Cost
A squashed baked bean	1p
A shark-infested aubergine	13p
Two used tea bags	8p
Half a clothes peg	2p

EXAMPLE: Katherine has 5 pet monsters. Their heights are shown in the table below. What is the mean height of the monsters?

Monster	Height
Bone Crunching Balthazar	800 cm
Fearsome Lord Frederick	420 cm
THE MIGHTY GIANT	10 cm
Eeepijeek the Ancient	200 cm
Tracey	70 cm

Add up the numbers:

800 + 420 + 10 + 200 + 70 = 1500

There are 5 numbers, so divide the total by 5: 1500 ÷ 5 = 300

So the mean height is 300 cm.

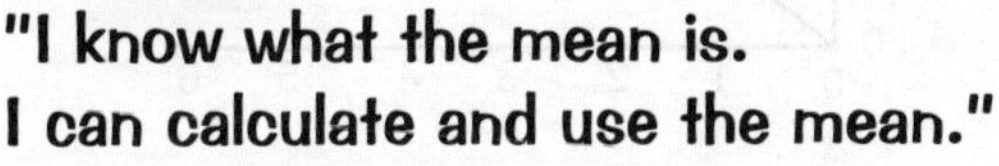

"I know what the mean is.
I can calculate and use the mean."

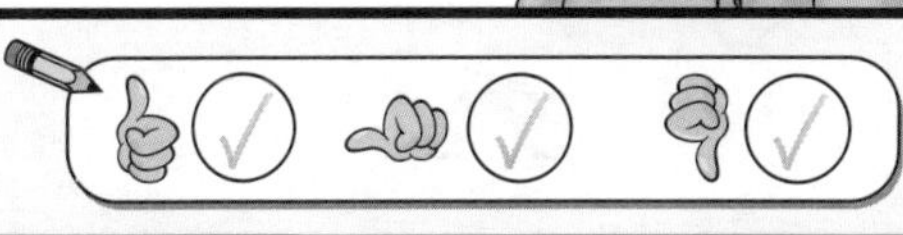

Practice Questions

Start off with the **green** questions — they're the easiest ones.
The **blue** ones are a bit harder, and the **pink** ones are the hardest.

1 The pie chart shows the drinks drunk by workers in an office in a week.

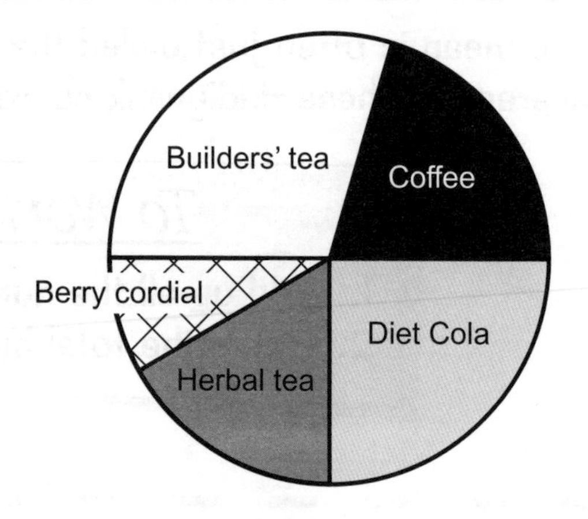

a) Which drink was drunk the most?

b) Which drink made up a quarter of the total drinks?

c) Which drink was drunk the least?

2 The line graph shows how the value of a car changes with its age.

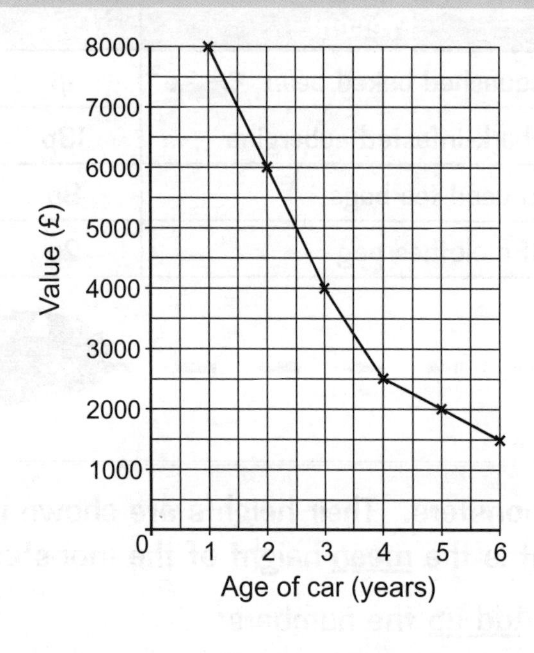

a) What happens to the value of the car as it gets older?

b) What is the value of the car when it is a year old?

c) What is the value of the car when it is 4 years old?

d) What was the mean value of the car over the 6 years?

3 The line graph below is a conversion graph for miles and kilometres.

a) What is 4 km in miles?

b) How many kilometres is 3.5 miles?

c) How many miles is 7 km?

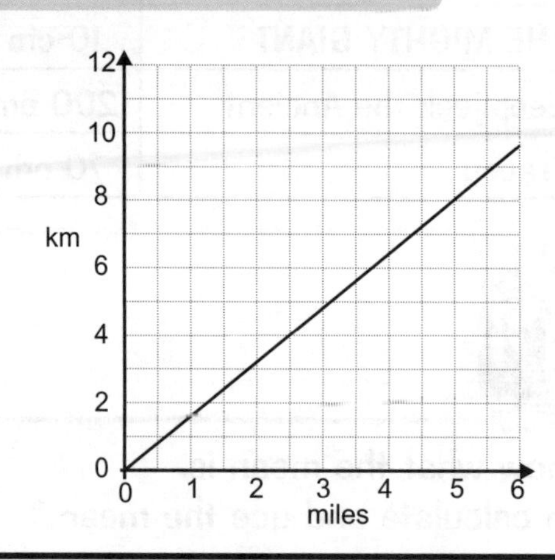

Practice Questions

4 The pie chart shows the favourite sandwich fillings of a class of 36 children.

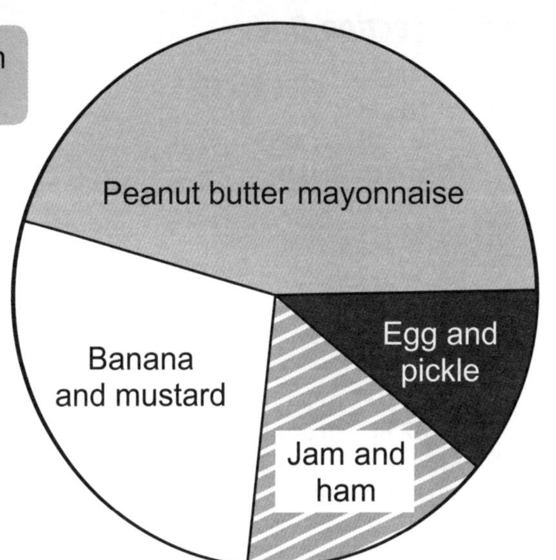

a) What was the most popular filling?

b) How many children said that egg and pickle was their favourite filling?

c) How many children said that banana and mustard was their favourite filling?

5 The scores of 6 dogs in a dog show are recorded in the table below. Mitzi's score is missing. If the mean score was 7, what was Mitzi's score?

Name	Percy	Jolly	Sneezy	Mitzi	Lulu	Wayne
Score	8	9	7		6	5

6 The speed of a car was measured every 3 seconds for 15 seconds. The results are shown in the table. Show these results in a line graph.

Time (seconds)	Speed (miles per hour)
0	0
3	35
6	65
9	90
12	105
15	115

7 180 people were asked what their favourite colour is. The results are shown in the table below. Draw a pie chart to show this information.

Colour	Number of people
Green	24
Red	40
Yellow	34
Purple	30
Blue	52

Answers

Page 6 — Section One

1) a) 100 000
   b) 23 163 000
2) a) From 1 to 0 is 1 °C
   From 0 to –9 is 9 °C
   1 + 9 = **10 °C**
   b) 10 °C
   c) –5 °C
3) Heaton: 13 °C
   Nippiham: 11 °C
   Chillbeck: 8 °C
4) a) 4 075 017 m around the Equator
   4 007 860 m around the poles
   b) Around the poles is shortest.
   c) 4 010 000 m

Pages 14-15 — Section Two

1) 28.8 + 71.1 ≈ 30 + 70 = **100**
2) a) E.g. 24
   b) E.g. 15
   c) E.g. 18
   List the times tables of both numbers and look for a number that's in both lists.
3) **Yes**. 53 only divides exactly by 1 and itself.
4) 7 goes into 45 six times with remainder 3.
   So 45 ÷ 7 = $\mathbf{6\frac{3}{7}}$.
5) The factors of 16 are 1, 2, 4, 8 and 16.
   The factors of 28 are 1, 2, 4, 7, 14 and 28.
   So their common factors are **1**, **2** and **4**.
6) Round 22.5 to numbers that are easily divided by 3.
   22.5 is between 21 and 24.
   21÷ 3 = 7
   24 ÷ 3 = 8
   So the answer is between **7** and **8**.
7) 8.9 × 11.7 ≈ 9 × 12 = **108**
   The answer should be a bit less than 108, because you rounded both numbers up.
   So Guy's answer is likely to be **wrong**.
8) a) 6 ÷ 2 = 3
   3 + 4 = **7**
   b) 2 + 4 = 6
   6 ÷ 6 = **1**
   c) 2 × 4 = 8
   6 + 8 = **14**
9) a)

$$\begin{array}{r} 4523 \\ \times \quad 12 \\ \hline 9046 \\ +\,45230 \\ \hline \mathbf{54276} \\ {}^{1}\quad\quad \end{array}$$

   b)

$$\begin{array}{r} 1595 \\ \times \quad 24 \\ \hline 6380 \\ +\,31900 \\ \hline \mathbf{38280} \\ {}^{1}\quad\quad \end{array}$$

10) a) 3660 = 3000 + 600 + 60
    So 27 310 + 3000 = 30 310
    30 310 + 600 = 30 910
    30 910 + 60 = **30 970**
    b) 4200 = 4000 + 200
    12 692 – 4000 = 8692
    8692 – 200 = **8492**
11) 16 = 10 + 6
    Double 10 = 20
    Double 6 = 12
    So Charlotte has 20 + 12 = 32 fish.
    32 + 10 = 42
    42 + 6 = 48
    So they have **48 fish** altogether.

Answers

12) 37, 41, 43, 47 and 53.
Prime numbers are numbers that have only two factors — 1 and themselves.

13) Make £1200 a hundred times smaller — that's 12.
$12 \times 6 = 72$
Now make 72 a hundred times bigger — 7200.
So Larry will earn **£7200** in six months.

14) a)
$$\begin{array}{r} 577 \\ 11\overline{)6354} \\ -55 \\ \hline 85 \\ -77 \\ \hline 84 \\ -77 \\ \hline 7 \end{array}$$
So $6354 \div 11 =$ **577 r 7**

b)
$$\begin{array}{r} 224 \\ 14\overline{)3145} \\ -28 \\ \hline 34 \\ -28 \\ \hline 65 \\ -56 \\ \hline 9 \end{array}$$
So $3145 \div 14 =$ **224 r 9**

15) a) $49.6 \times 2.7 \approx 50 \times 3 =$ **150 km**
b) Both numbers are rounded up so the real answer should be **smaller** than the estimate.

16) **b)** $(15 - 3) \div 4$
Subtraction normally comes after division — if the subtraction needs to happen first though, there must be brackets around it.

17) a) $19 \div 3 = 6$ r 1
Anja can't buy part of a box, so you need to round the answer down to **6 boxes**.
b) $29 \div 8 = 3$ r 5
If James buys 3 boxes he will only have 24 pipes, so you need to round the answer up to **4 boxes**.

Pages 26-27 — Section Three

1) a) $\frac{4}{8} = \mathbf{\frac{1}{2}}$
Divide the top and bottom by 4.
b) $\frac{18}{24} = \mathbf{\frac{3}{4}}$
Divide the top and bottom by 6.
c) $\frac{10}{25} = \mathbf{\frac{2}{5}}$
Divide the top and bottom by 5.

2) a) $\frac{1}{2} = \mathbf{\frac{3}{6}}, \frac{2}{3} = \mathbf{\frac{4}{6}}$
6 is a common multiple of 2 and 3.
b) $\frac{1}{3} = \mathbf{\frac{4}{12}}, \frac{3}{4} = \mathbf{\frac{9}{12}}$
12 is a common multiple of 3 and 4.
c) $\frac{7}{8} = \mathbf{\frac{21}{24}}, \frac{1}{6} = \mathbf{\frac{4}{24}}$
24 is a common multiple of 8 and 6.

3) a) $\frac{1}{12} + \frac{5}{6} = \frac{1}{12} + \frac{10}{12} = \frac{1+10}{12} = \mathbf{\frac{11}{12}}$
b) $\frac{3}{7} \times \frac{2}{5} = \frac{3 \times 2}{7 \times 5} = \mathbf{\frac{6}{35}}$
c) $\frac{4}{9} + \frac{1}{6} = \frac{8}{18} + \frac{3}{18} = \frac{8+3}{18} = \mathbf{\frac{11}{18}}$

4) a) **69.51**
b) **1.27**
c) **20.00**
Don't remove the two zeros after the decimal point, as you're asked to round to 2 decimal places.

5) a) $\frac{1}{3} \div 6 = \frac{1}{3 \times 6} = \mathbf{\frac{1}{18}}$
b) $\frac{4}{5} \div 6 = \frac{4}{5 \times 6} = \frac{4}{30} = \mathbf{\frac{2}{15}}$
c) $\frac{3}{11} \div 6 = \frac{3}{11 \times 6} = \frac{3}{66} = \mathbf{\frac{1}{22}}$

6) a) $\frac{2}{3} = \frac{8}{12}, \frac{3}{4} = \frac{9}{12}, \frac{7}{12}, \frac{1}{2} = \frac{6}{12}$
so the order is $\mathbf{\frac{1}{2}, \frac{7}{12}, \frac{2}{3}, \frac{3}{4}}$
12 is a common multiple of 3, 4, 12 and 2, so first make equivalents with 12 as the denominator (bottom number).
b) $\frac{5}{12} = \frac{25}{60}, \frac{1}{5} = \frac{12}{60}, \frac{2}{6} = \frac{20}{60}, \frac{3}{10} = \frac{18}{60}$
so the order is $\mathbf{\frac{1}{5}, \frac{3}{10}, \frac{2}{6}, \frac{5}{12}}$
60 is a common multiple of 12, 5, 6 and 10.
c) $\frac{2}{9} = \frac{4}{18}, \frac{1}{6} = \frac{3}{18}, \frac{1}{3} = \frac{6}{18}, \frac{7}{18}$
so the order is $\mathbf{\frac{1}{6}, \frac{2}{9}, \frac{1}{3}, \frac{7}{18}}$
18 is a common multiple of 9, 6, 3 and 18.

7) a) 12460
= **12460.0** to 1 decimal place
b) 4.192
= **4.2** to 1 decimal place
c) 857.05
= **857.1** to 1 decimal place

Answers

8) a) $1\frac{5}{12} = \frac{12+5}{12} = \frac{17}{12}$

$\frac{14}{12}$

$\frac{4}{3} = \frac{16}{12}$

so the order is $\mathbf{\frac{14}{12}, \frac{4}{3}, 1\frac{5}{12}}$

First, make all the numbers into improper fractions. Then find equivalents to make them all have a common denominator.

b) $2\frac{1}{5} = \frac{5+5+1}{5} = \frac{11}{5} = \frac{33}{15}$

$2\frac{2}{3} = \frac{3+3+2}{3} = \frac{8}{3} = \frac{40}{15}$

$\frac{37}{15}$

so the order is $\mathbf{2\frac{1}{5}, \frac{37}{15}, 2\frac{2}{3}}$

c) $3\frac{1}{3} = \frac{3+3+3+1}{3} = \frac{10}{3} = \frac{40}{12}$

$\frac{13}{4} = \frac{39}{12}$

$\frac{7}{2} = \frac{42}{12}$

so the order is $\mathbf{\frac{13}{4}, 3\frac{1}{3}, \frac{7}{2}}$

9) a) $2\frac{1}{4} - 1\frac{3}{4} = \frac{4+4+1}{4} - \frac{4+3}{4} = \frac{9}{4} - \frac{7}{4}$

(To make them into improper fractions.)

$= \frac{9-7}{4} = \frac{2}{4} = \mathbf{\frac{1}{2}}$

b) $1\frac{1}{3} + 3\frac{1}{2} = \frac{3+1}{3} + \frac{2+2+2+1}{2} = \frac{4}{3} + \frac{7}{2}$

(To make them into improper fractions.)

$= \frac{8}{6} + \frac{21}{6}$

(Equivalents with a common denominator.)

$= \frac{8+21}{6} = \frac{29}{6} = \frac{6+6+6+6+5}{6} = \mathbf{4\frac{5}{6}}$

Turn the answer back into a mixed number if you can.

c) $\frac{5}{9} \times \frac{2}{5} = \frac{5 \times 2}{9 \times 5} = \frac{10}{45} = \mathbf{\frac{2}{9}}$

Remember to simplify your answer where you can.

10) a) 5.84×5

$= 584 \times 5$, divided by 100

$$\begin{array}{r} 584 \\ \times \quad 5 \\ \hline 2920 \\ {\scriptstyle 4\,2} \end{array}$$

$2920 \div 100 = \mathbf{29.2}$

Check by estimating: $6 \times 5 = 30$

b) 9.7×5

$= 97 \times 5$, divided by 10

$$\begin{array}{r} 97 \\ \times \quad 5 \\ \hline 485 \\ {\scriptstyle 3} \end{array}$$

$485 \div 10 =$ **48.5 cm**

Check by estimating: $10 \times 5 = 50$

c) 8.22×5

$= 822 \times 5$, divided by 100

$$\begin{array}{r} 822 \\ \times \quad 5 \\ \hline 4110 \\ {\scriptstyle 1\,1} \end{array}$$

$4110 \div 100 =$ **£41.10**

Check by estimating: $8 \times 5 = 40$

11) a) $6.3 \div 3$

$= 63 \div 3$, divided by 10

$$3 \overline{)6\,3} \quad \text{answer } 2\,1$$

$21 \div 10 = \mathbf{2.1}$

Check by estimating: $6 \div 3 = 2$

b) $12.06 \div 3$

$= 1206 \div 3$, divided by 100

$$3 \overline{)1\,{}^{1}2\,0\,6} \quad \text{answer } 0\,4\,0\,2$$

$402 \div 100 = \mathbf{4.02}$

Check by estimating: $12 \div 3 = 4$

c) $34.89 \div 3$

$= 3489 \div 3$, divided by 100

$$3 \overline{)3\,4\,{}^{1}8\,9} \quad \text{answer } 1\,1\,6\,3$$

$1163 \div 100 = \mathbf{11.63}$

Check by estimating: $33 \div 3 = 11$

12) a) By converting to tenths: $\frac{3}{5} = \frac{6}{10} = \mathbf{0.6}$

By dividing: $\frac{3}{5} = 3 \div 5$

$= 3000 \div 5$, divided by 1000

$$5 \overline{)3\,{}^{3}0\,0\,0} \quad \text{answer } 0\,6\,0\,0$$

$= 600 \div 1000 = \mathbf{0.6}$

b) By converting to hundredths: $\frac{7}{20} = \frac{35}{100}$ $= \mathbf{0.35}$

By dividing: $\frac{7}{20} = 7 \div 20$

$= 7000 \div 20$, divided by 1000

$$\begin{array}{r} 3\,5\,0 \\ 20\overline{)7\,0\,0\,0} \\ -\underline{6\,0} \\ 1\,0\,0 \end{array}$$

$= 350 \div 1000 = \mathbf{0.35}$

c) By dividing: $\frac{7}{8} = 7 \div 8$

$= 7000 \div 8$, divided by 1000

$$8 \overline{)7\,{}^{7}0\,{}^{6}0\,{}^{4}0} \quad \text{answer } 0\,8\,7\,5$$

$= 875 \div 1000 = \mathbf{0.875}$

13) a) $\frac{12}{50} = \frac{24}{100} = \mathbf{24\%}$

b) $\frac{2}{10} = \frac{20}{100} = \mathbf{20\%}$

Answers

c) $\frac{3}{8} = 3 \div 8$
$= 3000 \div 8$, divided by 1000

$$8 \overline{)3^{3}0^{6}0^{4}0} = 0375$$

$= 375 \div 1000 = 0.375$
(To convert the fraction to a decimal.)
$0.375 \times 100 =$ **37.5%**
(To convert the decimal to a percentage.)

14) a) E.g. by converting them all to a percentage:
Adnan eats $0.61 \times 100 = 61\%$
Ben eats 58.5%
Cat eats $\frac{6}{10} = \frac{60}{100} = 60\%$
Ben eats the least, so has most sweets left.
b) **Adnan** eats the most, so has fewest sweets left.

15) a) $\frac{3}{4} + \frac{1}{5} = \frac{15}{20} + \frac{4}{20} = \frac{15+4}{20} = \mathbf{\frac{19}{20}}$
b) By converting to hundredths:
$\frac{19}{20} = \frac{95}{100} =$ **0.95**
By dividing: $\frac{19}{20} = 19 \div 20$
$= 19\,000 \div 20$, divided by 1000

```
    9 5 0
20|1 9 0 0 0
  - 1 8 0
      1 0 0
```

$= 950 \div 1000 =$ **0.95**
c) 0.17×5
$= 17 \times 5$, divided by 100

```
   1 7
×    5
   8 5
   3
```

$85 \div 100 = 0.85$, less than 0.95,
so **yes, he has enough left**.
Or, you could do $0.95 \div 5 = 0.19$. 0.19 is greater than 0.17, so yes, he has enough left.

Pages 34-35 — Section Four

1) $84 \div 7 =$ **12p**
2) $13 \times 5 =$ **65**
3) 10% of $80 = 80 \div 10 = 8$
So $20\% = 8 \times 2$
= **16 blue hairbands**
4) a) $12 \div 4 = 3$ times as many eggs.
3×1 lemon = **3 lemons**.
b) The recipe is for 2 people.
$20 \div 2 = 10$
$1 \times 10 =$ **10 lemons**
$4 \times 10 =$ **40 eggs**
5) The ratio is 8 chocolate bars to 2 free keyrings (8:2).
24 is 3 lots of 8 chocolate bars.
So $3 \times 2 =$ **6 keyrings**.
6) $28 \div 7 = 4$
$4 \times 2 =$ **8 cans** of paint are pink.
7) a)
b) Top of original shape = 3 squares
Top of enlarged shape = $3 \times 6 =$ **18 squares**
8) Scale factor:
enlarged length ÷ original length
$= 70 \div 7 =$ **10**
9) 10% of 240
$= 240 \div 10 = 24$
60% of 240
$= 24 \times 6 = 144$
5% of 240
$= 24 \div 2 = 12$
$144 + 12 =$ **156 orange flavoured biscuits**
10) Find 10% of 360°
$= 360° \div 10 = 36°$
Find 50% of 360°
$= 36° \times 5 = 180°$
Find 5% of 360°
$= 36° \div 2 = 18°$
Add them together
$180° + 18° =$ **198°**
11) There are 3 shares of gold coins in total.
For every 2 shares Penny gets, Luc gets 1 share.
So $150 \div 3 = 50$ gold coins (for 1 share)
$50 \times 2 = 100$ gold coins (for 2 shares)
Penny gets 100 gold coins, Luc gets 50 gold coins.
Remember, you can check your answer by adding the amounts and seeing whether you get the original total: $100 + 50 = 150$.

Answers

12) First convert both the amounts into pence, so £3.00 × 100 = 300p and £2.00 × 100 = 200p.
Charlie's ice cream
$\frac{75}{300} \overset{\div 3}{=} \frac{25}{100}$ = 25% discount
Johnny's ice cream
$\frac{40}{200} \overset{\div 2}{=} \frac{20}{100}$ = 20% discount
Charlie is giving the biggest percentage discount.

13) They share the raisins in the ratio 3:2.
There are 5 shares of raisins in total.
For every 3 shares that Hati gets, Dom gets 2 shares.
So Hati has $\frac{3}{5}$ = 15 of the total raisins and Dom has $\frac{2}{5}$ of the total raisins.
1 share = 15 ÷ 3 = 5 raisins
So Dom gets 5 × 2 = **10 raisins**.

Pages 40-41 — Section Five

1) 11 + 5 = **16**
16 + 5 = **21**
21 + 5 = **26**

2) a) 9 – 5 = 4
The rule is **add 4**.
b) 17 is the 4th term, so you need to add 4 3 more times.
17 + 4 + 4 + 4 = **29**

3) Lucy has £24, which is 4 times more than Jenny.
So 4△ = 24
Get △ on its own by dividing both sides by 4.
△ = 24 ÷ 4 = **£6**

4) Number of pens = 5 × Number of staff
Number of pens = 5 × 12 = **60**
You just need to substitute the number into the formula.

5) Possible answers are:
a = **1**, b = **4**
a = **2**, b = **3**
a = **3**, b = **2**
a = **4**, b = **1**

6) The rule to get to the next term is 'add 2'.
To get to the sixth day, add 2 three more times.
So 8 + 2 + 2 + 2 = **14**

7) Number of cows = 4 × Number of chickens

8) Volume = ½ × Base × Height × Length
Volume = ½ × 4 × 3 × 4
Volume = 2 × 3 × 4
Volume = **24 cm³**
You could also work out the volume of the shape first, then halve it. 4 × 3 × 4 = 48
48 ÷ 2 = 24 cm³.

9) Let the number of postcards be P.
21 + 12 = 33
Then 3P – 12 = 21
3P = 21 + 12
3P = 33
Get P on its own by dividing both sides by 3.
P = 33 ÷ 3 = **11**
Work backwards to get the answer — John triples the number then takes 12, so add 12 then divide by 3.

10) (4 × bowl) + (4 × plate) = 36
(4 × 4) + (4 × plate) = 36
16 + (4 × plate) = 36
4 × plate = 20
plate = 20 ÷ 4 = 5
So 1 plate costs **£5**

Answers

11) The difference between 13 and 1 is $13 - 1 = 12$
There are 3 steps to get from 13 to 1 in the sequence, so you subtract ☆ 3 times.
3☆ = 12
Get ☆ on its own by dividing by 3.
So ☆ = 12 ÷ 3 = 4
So the rule is "take 4".
The missing terms are:
$13 - 4 =$ **9**
$9 - 4 =$ **5**

12) $A + B + B + C + C = 14$
$A + B + B + 3 + 3 = 14$
$A + B + B + 6 = 14$
$A + B + B = 8$
$A + 2B = 8$
Substitute in a value for A:
Try $A = 2$
So $2 + 2B = 8$
That gives $2B = 6$
So $B = 3$
So a possible pair of values is **A = 2** and **B = 3**.
Other possible values are:
A = 4 and **B = 2**
A = 6 and **B = 1**

Pages 48-49 — Section Six

1) 1 l = 1000 ml
So 1056 ml = 1056 ÷ 1000 = **1.056 litres**

2) a) Area = ½ × 4 × 8 = **16 m²**
b) Area = 5 × 7 = **35 mm²**

3) The missing lengths are 2 cm, 3 cm and $6 - 1 - 2 = 3$ cm.
Perimeter = 2 + 6 + 2 + 2 + 3 + 1 + 3 + 3 = **22 cm**

4) 8 km ≈ 5 miles
32 km = 32 ÷ 8 = 4, 4 × 5 = 20 miles.
So **Tom runs the furthest**.
Here, it's easier to change the kilometres into miles rather than the miles into kilometres.
Do the conversion that's easiest — you just need both numbers in the same units.

5) 1 m = 100 cm
1.65 m = 1.65 × 100 = 165 cm
So the sunflower is 165 – 143 = **22 cm taller**.

6) The shape is made up of 12 cubes. Each cube is 1 cm³ so the volume of the shape is **12 cm³**.

7) 1 kg = 1000 g
Mass of box of chocolates = 0.1 × 1000 = 100 g
Mass of the empty box = 0.025 × 1000 = 25 g.
Mass of the 5 chocolates without the box = 100 – 25 = 75 g.
So the mass of one chocolate = 75 ÷ 5 = **15 g**.

8) 1 week = 7 days
1 day = 24 hours
So 1 week = 7 × 24 = **168 hours**.

9) Volume = Height × Length × Width
= 2 × 3 × 4 = **24 m³**

10) Area of rectangle (ignoring removed triangles) = 7 × 5 = 35 cm²
Area of one triangle = ½ × 2 × 2 = 2 cm²
Area of four triangles = 4 × 2 = 8 cm²
Area of quilt piece = 35 – 8 = **27 cm²**

11) Volume = Height × Length × Width
Volume of bead (no hole) = 3 × 4 × 3 = 36 cm³
Volume of hole = 1 × 4 × 1 = 4 cm³
Volume of plastic = 36 – 4 = **32 cm³**

12) a) Find missing length first:
Area = Base × Height = 5 × H = 15 cm²
5 × 3 = 15, so the height must be 3 cm.
So perimeter = 5 + 3 + 5 + 3 = **16 cm**
b) Area = 15 × 1 = 15 cm²

15 cm
1 cm

Perimeter = 15 + 1 + 15 + 1 = **32 cm**

Answers

Pages 60-61 — Section Seven

1) E.g.

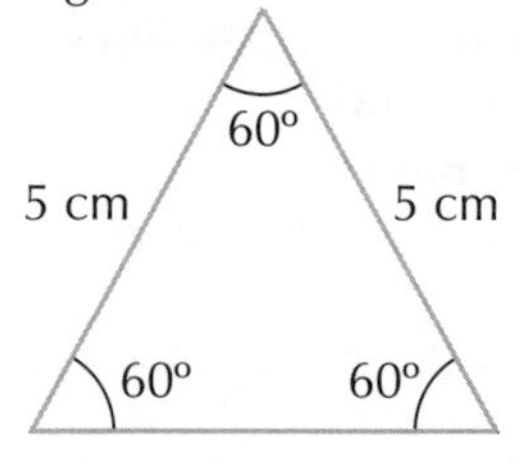

Not drawn to scale.

2) E.g.

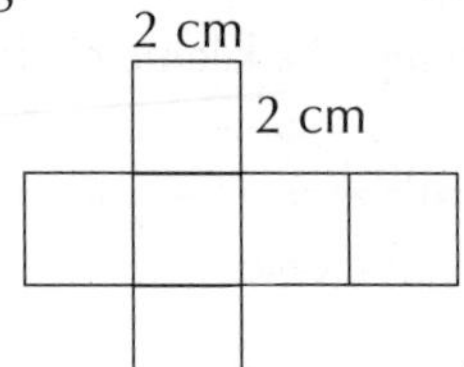

Not drawn to scale.

Make sure you use a ruler to measure and draw your net. The sides of each square should be 2 cm and each angle should be a right angle.

3) $90° + 48° + y = 180°$
So $138° + y = 180°$
$y = 180° - 138$
$y = \mathbf{42°}$
Remember that the angles in a triangle add up to 180°.

4) a) $d = 2 \times r$
$20 = 2 \times r$
$20 = 2 \times 10$
So $r =$ **10 cm**
b) the circumference

5) In a regular polygon, all the exterior angles are the same and can be found using the formula:
Exterior angle $= \frac{360°}{n} = \frac{360°}{6} = \mathbf{60°}$
All the interior angles are the same and can be found using the formula:
Interior angle = 180° – exterior angle
$= 180° - 60° = \mathbf{120°}$

6) a) (6, 2)
b)

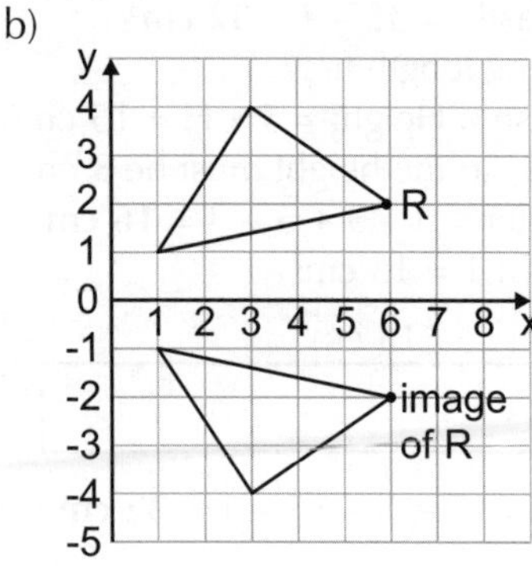

c) (6, -2)

7) a)

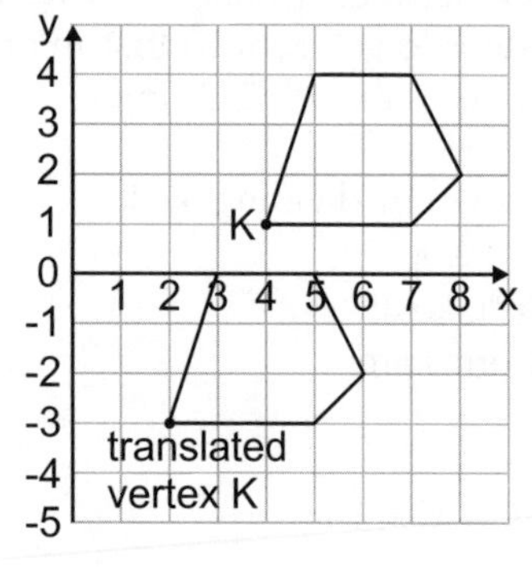

b) (2, -3)

8)

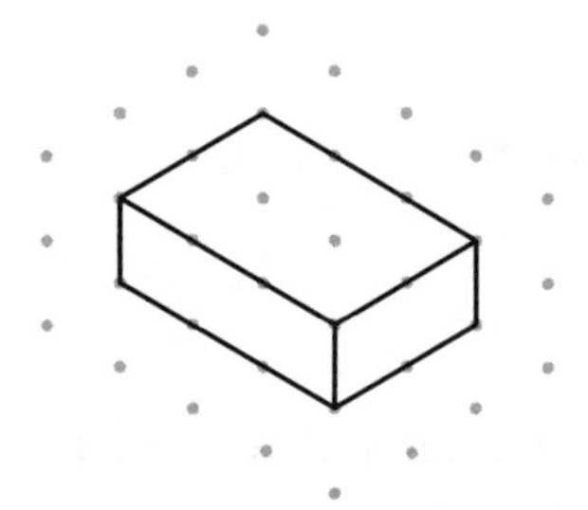

9) Parallelograms have two pairs of equal angles and the angles in a quadrilateral add up to 360°, so $123° + 123° + x + x = 360°$.
$246° + 2x = 360°$
$2x = 114°$
$x = \mathbf{57°}$
x + x is the same as 2x.

10) n and p are equal as they are vertically opposite angles, so p = **20°**.
Angles on a straight line add up to 180°.
m and n are on a straight line.
So $m + n = 180°$
$m + 20° = 180°$
$m = \mathbf{160°}$
m and o are equal as they are vertically opposite angles, so o = **160°**.

11) Point C is horizontally level with the point at coordinate (1, 2) — so they must have the same y-coordinate. It's 2. The kite is symmetrical. So the horizontal distance between point C and (–1, 4) is the same as the horizontal distance between (1, 2) and (–1, 4).
Look at the x-coordinates.
1 is two units to the right of –1.
So the x-coordinate of C must be two units to the left of –1.
So C has coordinates **(–3, 2)**.

Answers

Pages 66-67 — Section Eight

1) a) Builders' tea
   b) Diet Cola
   c) Berry cordial

2) a) As the car gets older its value decreases.
   b) £8000
   Find 1 year on the bottom axis, draw a line straight up until you reach the line, then change direction and draw a line straight across to the other axis. The number there (8000) is the value of the car.
   c) £2500
   d) Add up the value of the car for each year:
   8000 + 6000 + 4000 + 2500 + 2000 + 1500 = £24 000
   Divide the total by the number of values:
   24 000 ÷ 6 = **£4000**

3) a) 2.5 miles
   b) 5.5 - 5.8 km
   c) 4.3-4.4 miles
   The answer may be between two of the numbers on the axis. When this happens you need to estimate what the answer is.

4) a) Peanut butter mayonnaise
   b) Measure the angle of the sector: 40°
   Turn it into a fraction of the chart:
   E.g. $\frac{40}{360} = \frac{4}{36} = \frac{1}{9}$
   Find this fraction of the total number of children: $\frac{1}{9} \times 36 = 4$
   So **4 children** said that egg and pickle was their favourite filling.
   c) Measure the angle of the sector: 100°
   Turn it into a fraction of the chart:
   E.g. $\frac{100}{360} = \frac{10}{36} = \frac{5}{18}$
   Find this fraction of the total number of children: $\frac{5}{18} \times 36 = 10$
   So **10 children** said that banana and mustard was their favourite filling.

5) There are 6 dogs and the mean score is 7, so the total score of the 6 dogs added together is 6 × 7 = 42.
   The scores in the table added together are:
   8 + 9 + 7 + 6 + 5 = 35.
   So Mitzi's score is 42 – 35 = **7**

6) 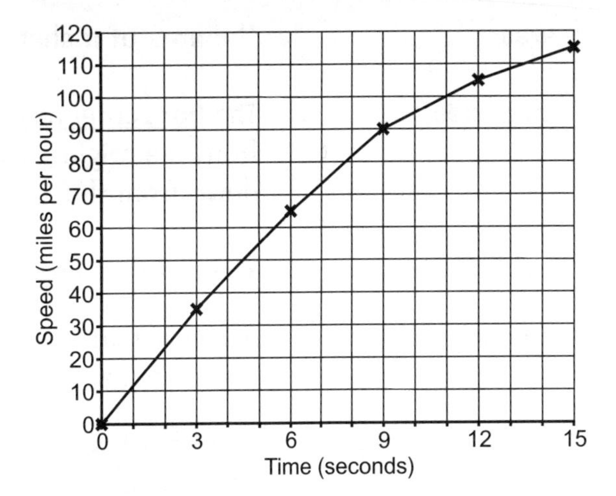

Remember to label your axes and to include units in the labels.

7) Total number of people = 180
   The multiplier = 360 ÷ 180 = 2
   So each person is represented by 2°.

Colour	Number of people	Angle
Green	24	24 × 2 = 48°
Red	40	40 × 2 = 80°
Yellow	34	34 × 2 = 68°
Purple	30	30 × 2 = 60°
Blue	52	52 × 2 = 104°

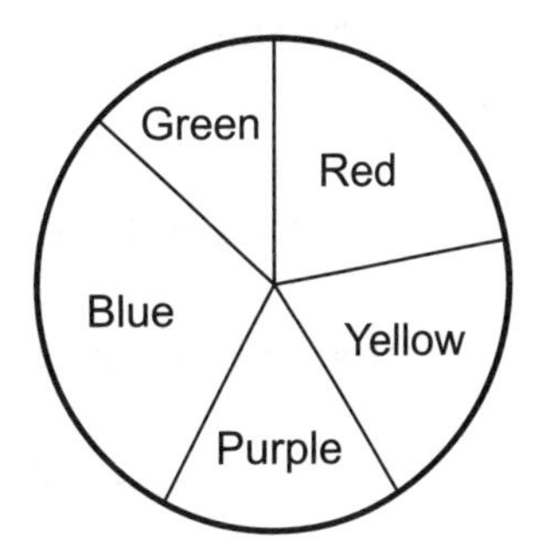

Glossary

area	The area of a shape is the amount of surface it covers.
axis/axes	The horizontal axis (x axis) is the line that goes across a graph or chart from the origin. The vertical axis (y axis) is the line that goes up and/or down from the origin. Axes is the word for more than one axis.
circumference	The distance around the edge of a circle. (The perimeter of a circle.)
common factor	A factor that is shared by two or more numbers. For example, 4 is a common factor of 8 and 12.
common multiple	Multiples that two or more numbers share. For example, multiples of 3 are 3, 6, 9, 12, 15... Multiples of 5 are 5, 10, 15... 15 is a common multiple of 3 and 5.
conversion graph	A line graph that lets you convert between different units. For example, from kilometres to miles, or miles to kilometres.
coordinates	They tell you the position of a point on a grid. For example, (3, 4) means 3 units to the right of the origin and 4 units up. The first number is the x-coordinate and the second number is the y-coordinate.
cubic centimetre, cm^3	A unit for measuring volume. A cube with sides 1 cm long.
decimal places	The places in a number to the right of the decimal point. For example, the number 4.56 has 2 decimal places.
decimal point	The dot you write in a decimal number. It comes between the units and the tenths.
degrees, °	The units used to measure angles.
denominator	The bottom number of a fraction.
diagonal	A diagonal line is the line joining two corners that aren't next to each other in a shape. People also say 'a diagonal line' to mean a sloping line (not horizontal or vertical).
diameter	The distance across a circle, passing through the centre.
difference	The difference between two numbers is the bigger number – smaller number.
enlargement	An enlargement is where a shape gets bigger using a scale factor.
equilateral triangle	A triangle with all sides the same length (and all angles 60°).

Glossary

equivalent	Something that has the same value but looks different. For example, $\frac{1}{2}$ and $\frac{2}{4}$ are equivalent fractions.
estimate	An estimate is a sensible guess at the answer. You can use rounding to help you estimate answers.
exterior angle	An angle between the side of a shape and a line extended from the next side.
face	A side of a solid shape. Faces can be flat, as on cubes. They can also be curved, as on cylinders.
factor	A whole number that divides exactly into another whole number. For example, the factors of 6 are 1, 2, 3 and 6.
formula	A formula tells you how to work out one quantity when you know a different quantity. For example, you can work out the total number of legs in a group of ants by using the formula: Total number of legs = number of ants × 6.
horizontal	Going across. This line is horizontal. → ______ Shelves and table tops are horizontal.
hundredths	The second digit after the decimal point. One hundredth is written 0.01 or $\frac{1}{100}$.
image	A transformed shape.
improper fraction	A fraction with a numerator bigger than its denominator, for example, $\frac{9}{7}$.
interior angle	An angle inside a shape between two adjacent sides.
irregular polygon	In an irregular polygon, the sides are not all equal lengths and all angles are not the same.
isometric paper	Dotty paper used to draw 3D shapes.
isosceles triangle	A triangle with two equal sides and two equal angles.
line graph	A graph with points that are joined by lines.
line of symmetry	If you fold a shape along a line of symmetry, the two halves fit exactly on top of each other. It's the same thing as a mirror line.
mean	One kind of average. To work out the mean, you add up all the values then divide by the total number of values.
mirror line	The same as a line of symmetry.

Glossary

mixed number	A mixed number has a whole-number part and a fraction part, for example, $3\frac{1}{10}$.
multiple	Multiples are the answers in a times table. E.g. multiples of 6 are 6, 12, 18... They go on forever because you can always multiply by higher numbers.
net	A 2D shape that will fold up to make a solid shape.
numerator	The top number of a fraction.
origin	Where the two axes of a graph meet. It has the coordinates (0, 0).
parallel	Parallel lines, faces and edges are always the same distance apart. They will never meet or cross.
partition	Split a number up. You can partition numbers in many ways. For example, 173 = 100 + 70 + 3 or 173 = 150 + 20 + 3.
perimeter	The distance around the outside of a shape.
pie chart	A circular chart that shows things as proportions. The angles of the sectors in a pie chart add up to 360°.
polygon	A 2D (flat) shape with straight sides.
prime	A prime number is a number that has exactly two factors: 1 and itself. For example, 2, 3, 5, 7, etc.
proper fraction	A fraction that's less than 1. The numerator is smaller than the denominator. For example, $\frac{2}{5}$ or $\frac{3}{4}$.
proportion	Another word for fraction. For example, 1 in every 4 is the same as ¼. It has other meanings too, but don't worry about them for now.
quadrant	Each quarter of a grid. There are 4 quadrants altogether.
quadrilateral	A flat shape with 4 straight sides.
radius	The distance from the centre of a circle to the edge.
ratio	A ratio is one way of comparing amounts. For example, if there are three apples and two oranges in a bowl, the ratio of apples to oranges is 3 to 2, written 3:2.
reflective symmetry	A shape has reflective symmetry if you can draw a mirror line on it.

Glossary

regular polygon	In a regular polygon, all the sides are equal lengths and all the angles are the same.
remainder	What's left over when you divide. For example, 7 ÷ 2 = 3 remainder 1. The remainder can be written as a number, a fraction or a decimal.
rounding	Finding a nearby number that's similar, but easier to use in calculations. For example, to round 27 to the nearest 10, you have to find the number that's nearest to 27 and a multiple of 10. 27 is between 20 and 30 but nearer to 30.
scale factor	The number each side of a shape is multiplied by in an enlargement.
sequence	A list of numbers or shapes. There is a rule or pattern that links each number or shape to the one before. For example, 3, 6, 9, 12... is a number sequence.
simplifying	Simplifying a fraction means making an equivalent fraction with the smallest numbers possible. For example, $\frac{6}{8}$ simplifies to $\frac{3}{4}$.
square centimetre, cm^2	A unit for measuring area. A square with sides 1 cm long.
tenths	The first digit after the decimal point. One tenth is written 0.1 or $\frac{1}{10}$.
term	Each number in a number sequence. For example, in the sequence 0, 2, 4, 6, 8, there are 5 terms.
thousandths	The third digit after the decimal point. One thousandth is written 0.001 or $\frac{1}{1000}$.
translation	When a shape moves from one place to another without rotating or flipping.
vertex/vertices	A vertex is a corner. Vertices is the word for corners.
vertical	Going straight up and down. Walls and flag poles are vertical.
vertically opposite angles	Pairs of angles made when two lines cross. Vertically opposite angles are equal.
volume	The volume of a shape is the amount of space it takes up.

Index